Routledge Revivals

Palestine

First published in 1942, *Palestine* is a brief history of Zionism, interspersed with a wealth of observation stimulation for the seeker of objective truth. The author develops his own theories of Jewish racialism, nationalism and colonization, and elaborates on the role of Britain with respect to Zionism in Palestine. He also expands on the binary of a spiritual Zionism and a territorial neo-Zionism stating that the former believed in peaceful coexistence with the Arab population in Palestine, while the latter is only invested in aggressive nationalism. The language used is a reflection of its era and no offence is meant by the Publishers to any reader by this republication. This book will be of interest to students of history, political science, international relations and geography.

Palestine
A Policy

Albert M. Hyamson

First published in 1942
by Methuen & Co. Ltd

This edition first published in 2022 by Routledge
4 Park Square, Milton Park, Abingdon, Oxon, OX14 4RN
and by Routledge
605 Third Avenue, New York, NY 10017

Routledge is an imprint of the Taylor & Francis Group, an informa business

© Methuen & Co., 1942

All rights reserved. No part of this book may be reprinted or reproduced or utilised in any form or by any electronic, mechanical, or other means, now known or hereafter invented, including photocopying and recording, or in any information storage or retrieval system, without permission in writing from the publishers.

Publisher's Note
The publisher has gone to great lengths to ensure the quality of this reprint but points out that some imperfections in the original copies may be apparent.

Disclaimer
The publisher has made every effort to trace copyright holders and welcomes correspondence from those they have been unable to contact.

A Library of Congress record exists under LCCN: 42020035

ISBN: 978-1-032-30974-3 (hbk)
ISBN: 978-1-003-30750-1 (ebk)
ISBN: 978-1-032-30975-0 (pbk)

Book DOI 10.4324/9781003307501

PALESTINE: A POLICY

by
ALBERT M. HYAMSON

With a Foreword by

SIR RONALD STORRS
K.C.M.G., C.B.E.

METHUEN & CO. LTD. LONDON
36 Essex Street, Strand, W.C.2

First published in 1942

PRINTED IN GREAT BRITAIN

FOREWORD

By SIR RONALD STORRS, K.C.M.G., C.B.E.

BEFORE INTRODUCING this book, I beg to re-introduce the author to the general public; and trust I shall be pardoned if I refer the curious to what I have said about him on page 434 of my *Orientations*.

There have been written recently two books deserving the earnest attention alike of Zionist, of non-Zionist and of anti-Zionist Jews, and of all Gentiles of sufficient intelligence and sympathy (seldom combined over this problem) to read with profit a sober and balanced presentment of Zionism. 'Aye: there's the rub.' For both Albert Hyamson in this *Palestine: a Policy* and Norman Bentwich in his *Wanderer between Two Worlds* represent the type of Jewish-Zionist author that tempers the keen wind of total Jewry to the shorn Gentile; by the faculty, almost as rare among Zionists as among their bitterest persecutors, of seeing the 'other man's' side to their own Question.

This dispassionate, *sine ira et studio* writing; this *festina lente* Fabianism, tolerable from a third party, from an opponent positively laudable, may gall and provoke the complete—not to say the extreme—Zionist with a revulsion almost of betrayal, by no means diminished by a precision and scholarship whose chapter and verse even where not specifically cited are always clearly implied.

Yet it would be a strange and a hard paradox for Jewry if the spiritual in total Zionism should ever become so heavily earthed over by the territorial that a Jew could be assailed by Jews for recording objective truth, with his honest opinions thereon. We have it from the Hippicus and Phasael of British Zion that, while facts are sacred (and none will suggest that they are not so treated here), comment is free.

'Come now, let us reason together, saith the Lord.' There lives no record of reply. The Old Testament is an incomparable gathering of supreme ethic, superb lyric and sublime oratory, but for drama, save in the noble mystery of Job—for Tragedy and Comedy, of which the essence is the other man's point of view, we must await the rise of Hellas. Jurists, scientists, industrialists— even artists—of an infinite objective receptivity in their own fields seem, so soon as they become Zionists, to be still obsessed by the 'intolerable honour' of having revealed monotheism: thou shalt have none other gods but me.

Albert Hyamson 'would describe himself as a Zionist, although most of his Zionist friends will resent the description. Unfortunately the whole subject of Britain and Jew in Palestine has been enveloped in exaggeration and beclouded in propaganda.' And again, 'In Palestine all men, and very many women also, are politicians, but the level of a statesmanlike outlook is extraordinarily low, according to Western standards. In choosing an object one never takes practicabilities into consideration: it is only one's wishes—and these are seldom moderate ones—that count': tragic results of a bimillenial divorce from political actuality.

This book is a brief and eminently manageable account

(rather than history) of Zionism, interspersed with a wealth of observation stimulating for the seeker after objective truth, though to others sometimes disconcerting, unsettling and provocative of that thinking feeling, so dreaded in advertisements. There is a fine and convincing analysis of the Jewish 'Mission', with a quotation from the pre-Christian Hillel which should be laid to heart by Gentiles throughout the world—and particularly throughout the continent of Europe. The author is not afraid to develop his own theories of Jewish racialism, nationalism and colonization. 'Biologically,' he observes, 'the Jews are certainly not a race'—any more than are the Aryans, from whose remote, linguistic relationship some people derived until the days of Nazism a vague satisfaction.

'Jewish nationalism,' he continues (with a boldness which does him credit), 'is in a sense the supreme instance of assimilation. . . . It is a movement to divest Jewry of its peculiar attributes and to make it "as other nations". . . . The Jewish Nationalists, the Political Zionists are in reality among the most assimilated of the Jews.' And he has the hardihood to reinforce this charge of assimilation—*Hitbolelut (Khas ve-Shalom)*—the unforgivable sin, with a quotation from the Rabbi Israel Mattuck: 'Modern Jewish Nationalism . . . is partly European nationalism applied to Jews, and partly the result of pressure on the Jews by Anti-Semitism. Jewish Nationalism and Anti-Semitism are two branches of the same tree . . .': something, after all of Herzl's original thesis.

'The revival of the Hebraic spirit does not depend upon the establishment of a certain number of colonies, but upon the establishment of a Jewish spiritual life in

Palestine.' Thus Ahad Ha'Am, thus Nahum Sokolow; but not thus the Rabbi answering me on the Cunarder. '*Ahad Ha'Am? Tsyoni ruhñi*'—spiritual Zionist! '*Bogéd*' —traitor! and not thus, I gather, the total discipline of the Palestine *Histadruth*. And certainly, such spiritual liberalisms involve a head-on collision with *Der Judenstaat*.

The author pointedly endorses the Baron Edmond de Rothschild's Jewish settlements in Palestine 'on lines that, while benefiting the new settlers, threatened the interests of no one else'. 'One consequence was that in later times when Palestine was the centre of upheaval, with the Arabs seething with fear and hatred of the Jewish newcomers, peace was seldom disturbed on the Rothschild lands where Jews and Arabs had for a generation learned to dwell together in amity.'

He does well to remind the British as well as the Zionist public that 'In their disappointment' with a celebrated White Paper 'Zionists exaggerated the decisions and read into the document meanings it did not contain' for a reason readily comprehensible to anybody with practical experience of Zion. 'Unfortunately in and of Palestine even more than elsewhere there is a tendency not to read or understand documents, but to accept the interpretation of parties more concerned in furthering their own point of view than in ascertaining or publishing the facts.' He acknowledges the fateful and ruinous results of the Zionist rejection of the Wauchope constitution: 'the Arab rising . . . came in April 1936, the disappointment over the failure of the Legislative Council and the apparently resolutely unfriendly attitude of the British House of Commons being undoubtedly among the contributory causes, if not the deciding factor.' He correctly appraises the Peel Report, with its admirably diagnosed premises and its hopeless conclusion and major recommendation: like one of the clever concertos of César Franck, the more studied the less respected. He sets his hope for Zionism in Arab Federation; partly for reasons of economic wisdom: 'The Jews of Palestine are dependent on foreign markets, and the nearest and most obvious and easiest attainable are those in the neighbouring lands.'

Modesty debars me from complacent enumeration of the passages in which his theses endorse those of *Orientations*. Even apart from those of the Gentile *Hoveve Zion* all over the world who feel and share the bitter agony of universal Jewry, few can reject the general proposition that the Arabs as a whole stand to profit from Jewish co-operation and prosperity. Only knowledge of the Land, sympathy with all its peoples and the wisdom which allows

> 'Old experience to attain
> Something like prophetic strain'

can determine the method and the degree. To such an understanding Albert Hyamson's book is a notable contribution.

RONALD STORRS,
xi. 1941.

PREFACE

THE APPEARANCE of yet another book on Jewry, the Jews, or Palestine, after the spate of recent years, requires perhaps an explanation if not an excuse. But the purpose of the following pages is somewhat different from that of most of the books that have previously appeared. An endeavour has been made to deal with the Palestine problem from a new angle, to relate British-Jewish relations and their connexion with Palestine, with the past, for these relations did not commence with the Balfour Declaration, nor did the British sympathy with Jewish aspirations in Palestine arise suddenly out of nothing a quarter of a century ago. Unfortunately the whole subject of Briton and Jew in Palestine has been enveloped in exaggeration and beclouded in propaganda. If this little book succeeds only in dissipating these clouds it will have served its purpose.

The writer would describe himself as a Zionist although perhaps many of his Zionist friends will resent the description. But the term Zionist, like the wider one Jew, has many meanings and shades of meaning. One can be a Zionist without being a nationalist, even an unaggressive one. The earlier Zionism, that which has had a far longer career than the Neo-Zionism of to-day, was none the less Zionist, even though it had no tinge of nationalism in the modern semi-aggressive sense. That Zionism was not based on a Jewish nation, whose existence in the modern sense it did not admit, but on the Jewish people. The earlier Zionism had no political connotation. It was no less successful on that account. It was certainly one of the instruments that kept Judaism alive and Jewry in existence. That early—it may be termed spiritual— Zionism still exists even though its voice is drowned by the more blatant shouts of a nationalism that differs from it in many respects. And as the earlier Zionism, which is a large part of Judaism, flourished for centuries before Political Zionism was conceived, it will not inconceivably survive political Zionism as a living force, for centuries. One more point. No one can point to any harm that the earlier Zionism has done to Judaism or to Jewry.

CONTENTS

	PAGE
FOREWORD BY SIR RONALD STORRS	v
PREFACE	xi
CHAPTER I: THE JEW AND THE MISSION OF ISRAEL	1

What is a Jew?: Jew: Hebrew: Israelite—The Mission of Israel—Israel among the Nations—Palestine, the Centre of Jewry.

CHAPTER II: MESSIANIC ZIONISM   16

The Religious Inspiration—The Darkest Hour Before the Dawn—False Messiahs—The English and the Jews—The Millenarians and the Judaizers—The Lost Tribes—Shabbathai Zevi.

CHAPTER III: THE BRITISH ATTITUDE   27

Jewish Settlement in Palestine—British Protection of the Jews—Shaftesbury: Palmerston: Finn—The Damascus Blood Accusation — Gawler's and other Projects — Laurence Oliphant—Edward Cazalet—Advocates of a Jewish State.

CHAPTER IV: PRACTICAL ZIONISM   46

Joseph Nasi and the Settlement of Tiberias—Montefiore and Jewish Settlement—Charles Netter—Abraham Benisch—Warder Cresson—Little Incentive to Emigrate —The Russian Persecution—'The Lovers of Zion'—The New Settlement—Edmond de Rothschild—Ahad Ha'Am.

CHAPTER V: POLITICAL ZIONISM   64

Theodor Herzl—The New Zionism—The Basle Programme—El Arish and East Africa—Herzl's Successors—The Ito Secession.

CHAPTER VI: THE BALFOUR DECLARATION 83

The War of 1914 — Chaim Weizmann — Influential British Interest—The Sykes-Picot Treaty—The Arab Question—The Balfour Declaration—Its Meaning—The Motives — Mr. Lloyd George's Views — Zionism and Bolshevism—The Anti-Zionists—The Arab Attitude—The Hogarth Message—The Supposed Price of the Balfour Declaration—The British Non-Zionists.

CHAPTER VII: ZIONISM IN PRACTICE 114

The Zionist Organisation—The Jewish Agency—Early Misfortunes—The War in Palestine—The Resumption of Immigration—The Jewish Development.

CHAPTER VIII: THE MANDATE AND ITS INTERPRETATION 126

The Terms of the Mandate—Need for Interpretation—The Churchill White Paper—Its Interpretation—The 1929 Outbreak—The Shaw Commission—The Passfield White Paper and the Macdonald Letter—Sir Arthur Wauchope's Régime—A Legislative Council.

CHAPTER IX: BRITAIN AND THE MANDATE 153

British Sympathy with the Jews—A Twofold Obligation—Jewish Friendliness towards Britain—Britain and the Arabs—The Influence of the Extremists—The British, the Scapegoat—Interference by the Amateur—Parliament and the Administration—Balfour on the Mandate—The Mandates Commission.

CHAPTER X: THE PEEL COMMISSION 168

The 1936 Rebellion—Sympathy of Foreign Arabs—A Royal Commission—The Mandate Unworkable—Partition of Palestine—Parliament: The League of Nations—Arab Opinion—The Zionist Attitude—The Technical Commission—End of Partition—An Abortive Conference—The New Government Policy.

CHAPTER XI: THE NEXT STEP 189

The Satisfaction of Competing Rights—Justice to Jew and Arab not Incompatible—Communal Autonomy—A Jewish National Home—Safeguards—A Federation—An Artificial Boundary—A Larger Customs Union, a Necessity—Immigration and Land—A New Arab-Jewish Co-operation.

INDEX 211

CHAPTER I

THE JEW AND THE MISSION OF ISRAEL

What is a Jew: Jew—Hebrew—Israelite: The Mission of Israel: Israel among the Nations: Palestine, the Centre of Jewry.

THE PROBLEM of Palestine is in part the Problem of the Jews. The latter problem is not a mere modern invention. It goes back to the beginning of the present era and even earlier. Remembering the past, one feels justified perháps in saying that the Jewish Problem will always be with us. But it is a problem that concerns not only the Jews, but almost, perhaps quite, as deeply the people in whose midst they live. It is to the interest of all, Gentile as well as Jew, that it should be solved and it can be solved only on just lines, fair to everybody. The Arab-Jewish Question is a part of the Jewish Question and if a way of resolving that can be found one step will be taken towards the greater solution.

Before it is possible, however, to give useful consideration to either the larger or the smaller problem we must clear our minds and define precisely what is meant by the term Jew, a term to which has been attributed almost as many meanings as there are continents in which it is used. *The Oxford English Dictionary* defines 'Jew' as 'A person of Hebrew race, an Israelite', and then continues 'Originally a Hebrew of the kingdom of Judah, as opposed to those of the ten tribes of Israel, later, any Israelite who adhered to the worship of Jehovah as conducted at Jerusalem. Applied comparatively rarely to the ancient nation before the exile, but the commonest name for contemporary or modern representatives of the race; almost always connoting their religion and other characteristics which distinguish them from the people among whom they live, and thus often opposed to *Christian*, and (especially in early use) expressing a more or less opprobrious sense.'

But this is clearly insufficient. There are Jews who are not of Hebrew race, even if the fact is ignored that within historical times there have been large admixtures of foreign blood. To say that a Jew is an Israelite carries one no distance. Again to say or to suggest that observance of or adherence to the Jewish religion is an essential qualification for a Jew would not be accepted by a very large and ever increasing number of persons who consider themselves almost passionately to be Jews and yet over whom the Jewish religion has no admitted influence. Moreover the other peoples label and consider many as Jews who have never seen the inside of a synagogue. The term Jew is very loose and is applied both to observers of the Jewish religion and even to those of another faith.

The *Jewish Encyclopedia*, which should perhaps be accepted as a better authority than *The Oxford English Dictionary* on this matter, says 'the word is often applied to any person of the Hebrew race, apart from his religious creed,' and the writer proceeds to use Hebrew and Israelite as synonymous for Jew. This definition is somewhat more embracing than that of *The Oxford English Dictionary*, but, as has been pointed out, it is not sufficient. A man not of Jewish race who has adopted Judaism is generally considered a Jew, yet he would be excluded by the encyclopædia's definition. The truth is that the word 'Jew' is used to connote three entirely separate ideas and in consequence much confusion, which could be avoided if separate terms were used, is caused and even further difficulties and impediments are put in the way of a clear and openminded consideration of a problem which is quite sufficiently difficult and complicated without any such avoidable obstacles.

That this question of terminology is not merely an academic one appears from an essay on 'The Primary Cause of Anti-Semitism' which was published by Mr. A. S. Schomer in New York in the year 1909. To him nomenclature was most certainly an element in that mental attitude towards the Jews which is generally known as Anti-Semitism. 'The names "Israel" and "Jew" impress the mind in a strikingly different manner. The mind realizes that the names "Israel" and "Jew" mean one and the same thing, yet its impression of these names is somehow different. The name "Israel" is regarded as something definite and normal, while the name "Jew" is considered as something vague, mysterious, puzzling.'

By the term 'Jew' as generally used to-day we understand either an adherent of the Jewish religion or a member of the Jewish race.[1] There is even arising in

[1] It may be argued that there is no Jewish race, but it is convenient to use the term which has acquired a definite and accepted meaning. Biologically the Jews are certainly not a race. The physical differences between Chinese, Yemenite, Abyssinian and European Jews are as great, greater, than those between Slavs and Latins and Teutons. The Sephardi of Spanish origin is as different from the Ashkenazi Jew of Poland or Russia as is the Spaniard from the Slav. Even psychologically there are great differences between the Jews of different countries. Only in Eastern Europe where the Jews lived for the most part in one great Pale, mental and intellectual even more than geographical, is there a common psychology and culture. There as everywhere the Jew, psychologically, culturally and physically, is the child of his environment. The Yemenite Jew is closer to the Arab than to the Jews of Europe; those of England or France to their fellow citizens than to their fellow Jews of other lands.

Palestine a third class, distinct from these two, which nevertheless considers itself Jewish. These are people who are neither of the Jewish faith nor of the Jewish race who yet live entirely in a Jewish environment, who marry with Jews and whose children will grow up ignorant that they are in any way different from the children of Jewish race with whom they play and next to whom they sit at school. We have in Palestine in these very early days of the Resettlement an assimilation of Gentile to Jew paralleled by the similar but necessarily far more widespread assimilation of Jew to Gentile in all the lands of the Diaspora. There are also baptized Jews, Hebrew Christians as they term themselves, who consider themselves members of the Jewish people although not of the Jewish faith. It is said that some of these made themselves evident at the Berlin Congress when it was thought that the future of Palestine would be taken into consideration. The International Hebrew Christian Alliance, when its constitution was drawn up, included among its aims 'To make it possible for Hebrew Christians, who may desire to do so, to share in the activities of Zionism, and to claim for them equal rights in terms of the Balfour Declaration.' Projects for Hebrew-Christian settlements in Palestine have been contemplated and even attempted.

Thus one term at present describes the adherent of the Jewish religion, the person of Jewish race and the member of the Jewish community or nationality, three entirely different ideas. And confusion necessarily follows. Once all three coincided, but that is no longer the case. It was not very long ago that all Jews, with very few exceptions, professed and practised the Jewish religion, were of the Jewish race—not necessarily a pure race but one practically so for many centuries—and lived together in self-contained communities. There were no Jews outside of these communities, we are justified in saying, and there were no non-Jews within them. Then a Jew was a Jew in all three senses. There was no need for a definition or for the discovery of alternative terms. That time has, however, passed and is unlikely to return in our generation. Before we can give proper consideration to the problem that is before us we must therefore define clearly what we mean by Jew, and state what terms we propose to use to designate those to whom this definition does not apply.

To Jew certainly and to Gentile also, the first idea that generally starts to the mind at the mention of the word 'Jew' is that of an adherent of the Jewish faith. He may be other things also, but he must be within the orbit of the synagogue if he is a Jew. Morris Joseph has expressed this view very clearly in his very valuable *Judaism as Creed and Life*. 'Judaism is something more than a badge, something more than a birthmark, it is a life. To be born a Jew does not declare any of us to be of the elect, it only designates us for enrolment among the elect.... "What makes a man a Jew?" is a question that is often asked. The answer is two things: membership of the Jewish brotherhood, and loyal fulfilment of the obligations which that membership imposes. At a time when religious observance among Jews as among non-Jews is falling into desuetude the word synagogue is used in the widest sense as representing any Jewish communal institution. A Jew must have some sort of connexion if not directly with a synagogue or Jewish religious organization, then indirectly through some Jewish lay institution. Otherwise he should not be termed a Jew. If he is what is known as a national Jew who looks forward hopefully and ardently to the creation in the near or distant future of a Jewish state or Jewish commonwealth or Jewish self-governing community either in Palestine or elsewhere, if the renascence of the Hebrew language is one of his ideals, he is more properly termed a Hebrew than a Jew. He may be both, for there is no reason why a Hebrew nationalist should not be a regular worshipper in synagogue, but if the synagogue and the many communal organizations of the Diaspora are nothing to him he is a Hebrew none the less, just as a professing Jew or one who takes his part in the management of his local Jewish community is a Jew even though he be definitely opposed to the nationalistic hopes and strivings of his fellows. And also just as a Jew need not be of Jewish parentage—he may have adopted Judaism—so any Gentile who adopts the Hebrew ideals and does his best to assimilate to a Hebrew environment may be a Hebrew even though there be not a drop of Israelite blood in his veins and he may never have seen the interior of a synagogue.

There remains the third class, that of members of what is generally known as the Jewish race. These had best be known as Israelites. They may also be Jews and Hebrews, or only Jews or Hebrews or neither. Lord Beaconsfield was an Israelite. He could not fulfil the conditions here laid down for a Jew or a Hebrew. All converts from Judaism to Christianity are Israelites although no longer Jews and almost certainly not Hebrews. In fact they often term themselves Christian Israelites. Opposite to them for instance are the Russian Slavs who have adopted Judaism and settled in Palestine. These are Jews and Hebrews but not Israelites and

THE JEW AND THE MISSION OF ISRAEL 7

their brethren who remained in Russia with no neo-Zionist inclinations became Jews but not Hebrews. They could not become Israelites. Most Jews and Hebrews will also be Israelites.[1] There are also the Russian Slavs who have gone half-way to Judaism, Sobotniki, 'Proselytes of the Gate', many of whom have settled in Palestine. These are not Israelites, hardly Jews. Under this nomenclature they should be termed Hebrews.

Before one proceeds to the main purpose before us there is one other matter, that at first sight might be considered irrelevant but is not really so, that may be briefly touched on. This is the so-called 'Mission of Israel' which to very many Jews and to a large number of non-Jews is the main if not the only justification for the survival of the Jew. To this end the survival of the Israelite is not sufficient. At the most it carries on the mission for a short time and in a diluted form. The survival of the Hebrew only helps towards the end in so far as the Hebrew movement—crystallized in Zionism—helps to preserve Judaism, in the preservation of which it is unquestionably a factor. But before it is possible to define the present of the Jew or the Hebrew or to forecast his future it is necessary to ascertain what exactly is the Mission of Israel, to what extent it has been fulfilled and what hope or expectation there is of its future complete or partial fulfilment.

The Idea of the Mission of Israel goes back to the day of Sinai when the Divine message was given through Moses: 'And ye shall be unto me a kingdom of priests

[1] The difficulty has been realized in other countries and in other languages, German, French, Polish, Roumanian, Russian, two, sometimes three, terms are employed to express the several ideas.

and an holy nation.'[1] And by the term 'priests' was meant, not ministers of a cult, masters of ceremonies, but teachers of and examples to all the other peoples, teachers not so much by precept as by example. Not individuals were to be selected as depositaries of the truth, to hold the lamp of virtue and right-doing to the world, but the entire people. The People of Israel was to light the way to the Millennium, the era of human perfection. It has even been said that the destruction of the Judaean state was a part of the Divine purpose of spreading Israel among the nations so that they might lead them to the true knowledge and worship of God.[2] 'The main hope of the fulfilment of Israel's vocation has always been centred in a gradual conquest of Man's minds and hearts by the silent influence of the Jewish life. The Jew's own fidelity to his religious and ethical ideals is at length to win the world's allegiance for them', said Morris Joseph in his *Judaism as Creed and Life*. A priest needs a congregation to whom to minister: a kingdom of priests, a nation of priests is commissioned to serve the other nations, all humanity. Again quoting Joseph: 'Thus Israel's mission, like his election, is purely religious. His is no worldly vocation, he has been called not for empire, for earthly power, for conquest, but to distribute the spiritual riches that have been entrusted to him. He has been called to be not the master, but the servant of mankind'.

It must not be thought that the Mission of Israel is to convert the World to Judaism. Judaism with its observances, its historical background, its rules and

[1] Exodus xix. 6.

[2] This view was expressed in a resolution adopted by the first Conference of American Jewish reformers in 1869.

regulations all tending to segregate the Jew, is essentially a national or communal religion as opposed to a universal one. In its present form, that is to say so long as it remains Judaism, it is impossible for this faith to draw its adherents from all sides. If it ever becomes universal it will cease to be Judaism, just as once before when its child Christianity, originally merely a reformed Judaism, made its appeal to the nations of the world, at the same time ceased to be the Jewish religion, the religion of the People of Israel.

The Mission of Israel is therefore not to act as missionaries of Judaism in the narrow sense, but to spread the essential truths of their faith and by both precept and example to propagate them among the peoples, and these essential truths have been defined as 'God, one, a spirit, the universal Father; man, heavenly in origin, free, responsible, endowed with the power of lifting himself to God in prayer and purity without extraneous aids.' This definition appeals perhaps more to the scholar, to the disputant, to the theological student. Translated into the language of the man in the street it means the white-heat passion for rightdoing, for justice, for mercy, for sympathy, for pity, for kindness. 'One law shall be to him that is home born and unto the stranger that sojourneth among you,' says the author of Exodus. 'He raiseth up the poor out of the dust, and lifteth the needy out of the dunghill,' says the psalmist. Character and righteousness are the keynotes of Judaism and these it is the mission of Israel to form and to preach.

The kernel of the Jewish teaching which it is the mission of Israel to spread throughout the world is the idea of justice, but of justice tempered by mercy. 'Love thy neighbour as thyself,' is a Christian doctrine, but it became Christian only through inheritance from Israel. Hillel, the Jewish teacher who flourished before the opening of the Christian era, taught the same when he said to a heathen enquirer: 'What is hateful to thee, do not unto thy fellow man; this is the whole law, the rest is mere commentary.' Brotherly feeling towards all others was demanded and therefore justice came first, so that a kindness to one might not be at the expense of another. Only when the interests of others had been safeguarded should justice be tempered by mercy. To perform this mission Israel had to be scattered among the peoples so that he might come into contact with them and everywhere point by the living example the way they should go. From this point of view the Dispersion was providential, for without it the Mission of Israel could never be fulfilled. Painful, acutely painful to the People of Israel and to its individual members, but the price or a part of the price the people had to pay for having been selected for its Mission, for the honour of being the Chosen People.

Judaism through its instrument, the Jewish people, fulfils another purpose in the moral history of mankind. Not only a minority but an almost infinitesmal minority in most lands, its mere existence breaks the overwhelming power of uniformity so harmful for the character of a people. The mere existence of the Jews shows Christendom that there may be more than one road that point to the ideal of perfection, that virtue is not necessarily the monopoly of one race or one faith and that following different roads we and our neighbours may still reach the same goal. This of course is not a new truth which the physical presence of the Jew is required to make manifest. The thinkers and philosophers of all times have realized this, but for the mass of the people things seen are mightier than things heard and one living Jew is more convincing than volumes of philosophy and history.

The existence of the Jew also helps to teach the Divine function of the protestant. Again the dead level of uniformity is broken up: the ever more heavy inertia that is inevitable when the rule is never broken, when an exception is unknown, is lightened. The changes that the passage of time always brings and the adaptations of practice and belief that must follow are forced into the consciousness by the existence of this ever present minority. If the Jew serves any purpose in the world it is that of the progressive and the reformer, the mind that realizes the changes that have imperceptibly come about and drives them into the consciousness of mankind. And this function again is not a popular one. The protester, the goad, the disturber of the serenity of uniformity, even if accepted as inevitable, is never universally liked. And since he is necessarily always in a minority, generally a very small one, his mere existence produces thorns in a bed that might, if he were as other people, be one of roses. The reformer is often crucified. That has been the fate of most of the prophets, but their prophecies have been none the less justified. If the Jewish people is looked on as the prophetic people, it will be realized that part of its mission is also to suffer.

As has been said, the Mission of Israel is a mission of example rather than of precept. It follows therefore that the Jew and the Jewish People, which is made up of Jewish individuals, need not be conscious of its mission to succeed or to perform its task. Rather the opposite, the less consciousness the greater the possibility of success.

No teacher who puts himself forward as a paragon to his disciples can ever succeed. No self-appointed teacher can gain a following. It is the disciples who must choose their teacher and in the same way a people if it is to gain influence, to become a light of the world, no matter how dim, must by its individuality, its own attraction, cause others to listen to and follow it. The most successful of missionaries is the one who is unconscious of his mission, who is unaware that he is not of the ordinary.

The Mission of Israel has now been defined, to spread throughout the world the idea of justice, of justice tempered by mercy. Is this mission completed? Has the whole world been converted? The answer is no, most emphatically no, an answer that no one can gainsay. Not centuries but millenia must still pass before the ideal of Isaiah can be attained. Not only has no nation been converted as a whole to righteousness, the People of Israel itself is still very far from the ideal. The inspirers, the teachers, the idealists of a people are, such is human nature, always an infinitesmal minority. No people can ever be a people of priests except vicariously through its few exceptional individuals. The People of Israel has in every generation produced these individuals, and to-day in ever increasing numbers the other peoples are doing so. But the number in the aggregate is very small. Their influence is growing, but it will be very long yet before the peoples of the world will be converted to universal justice, and until that day arrives the Mission of Israel will not be fulfilled. In the course of its Mission Jewry has already inspired or helped to inspire, directly or indirectly, many great movements for the benefit of mankind—Christianity, Islam, the Reformation, Puritanism, the modern humanitarian movement, socialism, the idea of a League of Nations. All of these owe much, in some cases very much, to the Hebraic character, the Hebraic point of view, and the list is not yet complete. Until it is, the Mission of Israel will not be finished. The Mission is in effect endless. 'This influence can never hope for a complete victory over the other influences at work on human society, which draw it in other directions,' wrote Ahad Ha'Am, the prophet of modern Zionism. 'It follows that there can be no end either to the Mission or to those to whom it is entrusted. The end can come, if at all, only when men cease to be men and their life to be human life.' 'In nature all forms die when their utility is over; in history peoples succumb when their work in and for the world is complete,' said Israel Abrahams. Centuries earlier, Jehuda Halevi realizing the same truth said: 'Israel is indestructible.' Judaism may be the sacred fire, but to hold it a lantern is needed and this lantern is the Jewish people. The preservation of this people is therefore a necessity to the present world. For the preservation of the People of Israel a Jewish environment, a Jewish concentration is essential. Otherwise the Jew perishes, absorbed into the environment that surrounds him.

Many forces have since the French Revolution been working towards the disintegration and disappearance of Jewry. Jewry may have had a Mission, but the Jews have for centuries been struggling hard to escape from that Mission. To the people it was a great honour, a sacred trust, but to the individuals who made up the people it was a terrible burden, one almost more than the individual could support. For two thousand years and longer Judaism, even Israelitism, has been in one sense a misfortune. The lot of the stranger is never a happy one, no matter how kind his hosts may be. The member of a minority, one who is an exception in one way or another to the people in whose midst he lives, is always a stranger and therefore never completely unselfconscious. And the self-conscious is never completely happy. Thus in Jewry, throughout the centuries of the Dispersion there has always been a longing for escape. Thousands, counting their descendants millions, did succeed in escaping and no one to-day can recognize these descendants. For those of them who survived escape was complete. But there was only one road of escape. Christianity, Islam, the Feudal system, the Guild system, all co-operated or succeeded one another in imprisoning the Jew (in the religious sense) in the Ghetto, moral and physical, or the Pale of Settlement. No one who professed Judaism could live outside of it. And those who escaped abandoned their Judaism. The end of the eighteenth century saw the beginning of the end of the ghetto system. But history moves very slowly and this end is not yet complete. Yet, despite the temporary widespread relapse into barbarism, a barbarism not limited to its treatment of Jews and Israelites, civilization continues on its march. The ghetto, the enforced segregation of the Jews, still exists, but compared with a couple of centuries ago there are many breaches in its walls. Judaism of to-day, the religion, is to a large extent a product of the ghetto and the undermining of a ghetto wall undermines it also. In the past the Jew who abandoned Judaism adopted Christianity. But Christianity also no longer has as wide an appeal even to its natural followers as it used to have. The spread of freedom of thought in matters of religion affects Jews as well as Gentiles, and without the bar of religion, in civilized society, the one safeguard against complete assimilation, which means the annihilation of Jewry not only as a religious community but also as a people, disappears. If Jewry is to be preserved, if its Mission is not yet complete, Judaism in the Diaspora is not enough. Judaism may be compared to the soul, with Jewry as the body. With the disappearance of persecution and the continued attraction of assimilation the days of Jewry in the Diaspora are numbered. To fulfil its mission it must find a centre elsewhere. From such a centre alone, in the absence of persecution, can Judaism in the Diaspora be kept alive for as long as we can foresee to-day that it will be needed. For this end a healthy in mind and body, free, happy Jewry is necessary. Thus all Jews to whom the survival of Jewry is of consequence should be and are Zionists.

CHAPTER II

MESSIANIC ZIONISM

The Religious Inspiration: The Darkest Hour Before the Dawn: False Messiahs: The English and the Jews: The Millenarians and the Judaizers: The Lost Tribes: Shabbethai Zevi.

ZIONISM MAY be said to be an essential part of Judaism. Without Zionism, without the hope that some day the Jewish people will be restored to, re-settled in, Palestine, Judaism is to an overwhelming majority of its adherents incomplete. It is true that many Western Jews, the so-called Liberal Jews or Reform Jews, have cut the return to Palestine out of their religion. To them Palestine does not exist, except as a matter of history and of geography. But the Liberal and Reform Jews comprise only an insignificantly small proportion of the Jewish people. By the term Jew is understood one who accepts the traditional Judaism in the broad sense. Those who subtract from it or add to it may be accepted as Jews but as Jewish sectaries. And belief in the return one day of the Jews to Palestine is one of the dogmas of traditional Judaism. Yet it must be admitted that the return in this religious sense is largely an academic one— a return some day as a precursor or an accompaniment of the millennium. To many Jews, perhaps to most

Jews, the Jewish people will return to Palestine in God's good time.[1] To them the restoration to Palestine and the appearance of the Messiah are parts of one whole that cannot be separated. To many to hasten that time, even to help towards it, is almost blasphemy. On the other hand among the ranks of the active Zionists, even of the political Zionists, there are many sincere religious Jews who know of no objection to their using all their efforts towards the re-settlement of Jews in Palestine, even to the end of the creation of a Jewish political state.

This promise of the Return to Palestine, partly mystical but not entirely so, for over long periods the hope was perhaps the principal force that kept the Jews from despair, permeated Jewish life, which in the medieval ghetto and the recent Pale of Settlement was almost coterminous with the Jewish religion. It entered into Jewish thought and Jewish belief at a thousand gates. It appears everywhere, in the ritual of the synagogue, in the prayers of the home and in the poetry of the people. 'If I forget thee O Jerusalem may my right hand forget its cunning' was not more real when uttered by the Waters of Babylon over twenty centuries ago in the first years of the exile, than it was in the Russian Pale of Settlement in the early years of this century and than it is to-day in countless Jewish homes. What the Millennium and the Second Advent are to millions of Christians, the return to Zion is to hundreds of thousands of Jews. And both are equally mystical—an end beyond the power of attainment by human effort unaided. The religious impetus was the great original one without which modern Zionism, the heir

[1] See M. Friedlander, *The Jewish Religion*, page 161.

of two thousand years, would never have come into existence.

Although it is Judaism, the Jewish religion, reinforced perhaps by the deeply-rooted human instinct to refuse to be driven, to react against the course that is being forced on it, that has preserved the Jewish people as an entity until to-day, there were many periods in Jewish history when the end seemed near at hand. Fortunately in the interests of the preservation of the people these periods never covered the whole of the Dispersion. In the times of the most poignant sufferings there were always regions in which Jewry was relatively unharmed. The Jews of Western Germany might be massacred almost to a man and woman by God-intoxicated soldiers of Christ, but those of Southern Europe were living in safety and comfort under the shadow of their vines and fig trees. When the time of those of Spain and Portugal came the Sultan in his wide dominions offered unlimited hospitality and opportunities to those who could escape. It was not an accident that Columbus sailing from Saltes to discover a new world—incidentally it may be mentioned that he had a number of Jewish victims of persecution with him and even he is said to have been the descendant of unwilling converts—overtook on his journey shiploads of Spanish Jews driven from the homes in which they and their ancestors had lived for fifteen hundred years. He sailed to discover America which to-day holds twenty-five times as many Jews as came under the ban of Ferdinand and Isabella.

Jewish history has never since the Dispersion been one. It has always comprised a number of local histories holding in common only the development or rather the lack of development of Judaism, the Jewish religion. The theologians, the doctors of Jewish law, and their stories have been common to the whole of Jewry. Otherwise each local Jewry has been immersed in its own affairs, which were generally too insistent to allow it to concern itself deeply with those of its fellow Jewish communities, aroused only to sympathy, as a rule helpless sympathy, expressible only in prayer, when some colossal misfortune overtook its co-religionists elsewhere. So far as the communities immediately affected by a major misfortune were concerned, they also, powerless to hold back the threatening sword, could find refuge only in the mystical world, in the hope or promise that the darkest hour was the prelude of the dawn, that when Jewry, that is the local community, appeared to be on the brink of annihilation, then at last the Millennium, the end of their age-long sufferings, was at hand. It was at these times, and in this soil, that the Messianic movements were strongest, the hope of, like the longing for, the Redemption keenest. Jewry that would be saved—for this was a cardinal principle of faith—could suffer no more keenly. Therefore the Messiah, the Redeemer, must be at hand. And in fulfilment, at these times a Redeemer, self-deluded generally, often arose proclaiming and generally believing himself to be the Messiah. These messiahs appeared even in Roman times, before the time of Jesus. There is a reference to some of them in Matthew and one of them, Theudas, is mentioned by name in Acts. A century after the Crucifixion Bar Cochba, bandit or rebel and messiah, wrested the Holy Land from the Roman yoke and held it for four years until his defeat and destruction. No later messiah arose in Palestine, but elsewhere, in the Diaspora, at one time in Crete, at another in Central Asia, at others in Sicily, in Portugal, in Turkey, in Poland, in Germany, messiahs arose when the fortunes of Jewry seemed to have reached a crisis. The latest of them all was as recent as 1889 when one Joseph Abdullah of Yemen in Southern Arabia proclaimed himself the Messiah ordained to bring the sufferings of Jewry to an end.

There was a curious connexion between this Pseudo-Messianic Movement and the re-settlement of the Jews in England and perhaps ultimately with British interest in the settlement of Jews in Palestine. Jewish communities which had settled in England on the invitation of William at the time of the Conquest and had contributed noticeably to the upbuilding of the country, were expelled by Edward I partly for religious, partly for economic reasons. Apart from a few occasional individuals, visitors or residents, there was no Jewish population in the country until the time of Cromwell. At the beginning of the seventeenth century Crypto-Jews from Portugal, forced converts, had begun to settle in the country and to conduct world-wide commercial activities from London. These were however nominally Catholics, although their Judaism was an open secret to the Protector and others. With correspondents in half the countries of the world and close business relations with all of them, Cromwell not only recognized the economic benefits these crypto-Jewish merchants brought to their new country, but took advantage of the services freely offered of political information of special value in the conduct of England's then developing foreign policy. For these reasons Cromwell, who was above all a statesman, was anxious to encourage the settlement of these Portuguese Jews in England.

MESSIANIC ZIONISM

This was for public reasons. But there were others that had little to do with politics or economics which, if they did not influence Cromwell himself, meant much for a large body of his supporters.

Among the many elements that went to make up the movement that culminated in the establishment of the Commonwealth some were even mystical. There were the Millenarians who expected the early completion of the Millennium and as a consequence the appearance on earth of the Messiah and the opening of a new era under his rule. One essential to this culmination was the return of the Jews to Palestine, a preliminary to which was their complete scattering over the face of the earth. Jews were known to be resident throughout the Old World, as then known. It was only the recently discovered New World, so it was believed, in which there were no Jews. Then came a curious story, brought by English missionaries from North America, of the identity of the American Indians with the Lost Ten Tribes and if any one doubted the genuineness of this identification, his doubts must have been dissipated by the almost simultaneous accounts brought to England by Manasseh ben Israel of the discovery by a Jewish traveller in South America of Jewish tribes among the Red Indians there. Manasseh ben Israel was the self-appointed emissary of the Jews of the Continent who, after preliminary talks with English diplomatists in Holland, had come to England to negotiate the re-admission of avowedly Jewish communities. His object was closely related to that of the Millenarians and their sympathizers. He also believed that the Messiah could not appear until the Jews were scattered in all the countries of the world. Convinced by the stories he had heard that they were to be found in America, knowing that Jews were scattered in all other regions of the three older continents, it seemed that if only Jews were settled in England also, prophecy would be fulfilled and the Messiah could set out on his journey. Manasseh had a personal interest or hope in this fulfilment. His wife claimed descent from King David, and as the Messiah, so it was foretold, would come of the same ancestry, perchance one of his sons would be the appointed one.

Among the many sects that flourished in England in the middle years of the seventeenth century there were others with close Jewish sympathies. There were the Judaizers who, without adopting Judaism, adopted many Jewish practices and took Jewish names. Some even went further and formally sought and obtained admission to the Jewish community. This was of course impossible in England where there were no avowed Jews and, if there had been, none foolhardy enough to begin openly making proselytes before their own position was regularized and while they were still in the country on sufferance. But these anxious proselytes sought other means of satisfying their ambition and went to Holland for the purpose, returning as fully accepted members of the Jewish Community.

The Millenarians and Judaizers were however not very important individuals. Manasseh ben Israel with his mystical hopes and beliefs stood almost alone in Western Jewry. But a powerful reinforcement came from an entirely unexpected quarter. Shabbathai Zevi was the son of a poulterer who later acted as agent for some English merchants at Smyrna, now Ismir, and was born there in 1626. Peculiar in his manner of life and

MESSIANIC ZIONISM

behaviour, he early came under mystical influences and adopted with fervency the belief then prevalent among Jews of the East that the year 1648 was to be the beginning of the Messianic age. He went so far as to reveal himself in that year, to a select group whom he had gathered round himself in Smyrna, as the expected Messiah. Shabbathai's father certainly did not go as far as his son in this direction, but he also lived in an atmosphere of expectation and there can be little doubt that his expectations were conveyed to his English business associates, carried by them to England and there communicated to English enthusiasts who had by other roads almost reached the same goal. There was of course no public appearance or acceptance of the Messiah in the year 1648, but neither the English nor the Jewish believers were dismayed on that account. A fanatic is never dismayed, or discouraged by any set-back or failure. If the Messiah did not appear in the year appointed, that was no reason why that year should not be the beginning of the appointed era, even though a very small and select body was given the privilege of the knowledge. Ultimately the year 1666 was appointed for the public appearance of the Messiah. In the meanwhile the number of Shabbathai's believers had grown manifold and his influence had spread through the length and breadth of the known world. Shabbathaism became the most powerful influence in Jewry and Jews went to astonishing lengths to show their acceptance of his claims. Jewish communities in the Diaspora began to wind up their activities in preparation for their return to the Holy Land. The Jews of Persia neglected to sow their lands, since they said they would no longer be there to reap the harvest. Merchants on the exchanges of Europe turned aside from their normal interests while the new phenomenon was discussed. Those, Jewish and Christian, of the North Sea ports wrote to their agents in the Levant for information. In Hamburg the people went to their pastor and inquired: 'We have almost certain accounts not only from Jews, but also from our Christian correspondents at Smyrna, Aleppo, Constantinople and elsewhere in the East that the new Messiah of the Jews does many miracles and the Jews of the whole world flock to him. What will then become of the Christian doctrine and the belief in our Messiah?' With such excitement on the Continent the welcomers of the Millennium in England could not remain untouched. By this time, the year 1666, a Jewish community had been openly and legally settled in England so that the repercussions of events in the Levant and on the Continent could no longer affect the question of the re-admission of the Jews. They helped however to keep alive in the minds of the English people an interest in the Jews and in Palestine, an interest that continued, practically without interruption, to the present day.

There remains to relate briefly the subsequent course of the Shabbathaian intoxication. At the beginning of the fatal year 1666, Shabbathai left Smyrna for Constantinople, believing or half believing that a miracle would happen and that he would be accepted as Messiah and as ruler of the whole world. On landing he was promptly imprisoned by order of the Sultan, but this seemed to dismay neither Shabbathai nor his followers. There was never yet a prophet who had not to pass through a period of tribulation before he could be accepted. And what was required of a prophet was still more necessary in the case of a messiah. The shackles of imprisonment pressed lightly on the illustrious prisoner. In his quarters in the Castle of Abydos he held a sort of court in the company of his queen, his wife Sarah, surrounded by his courtiers who lavished their wealth for the maintenance of his dignity, with crowds of visitors from all parts and with the unconcealed reverence and admiration of his gaolers and other Turkish officials. The accounts of his method of life spread through the Jewish world with the customary exaggerations and the cult of Sabbathaism increased rather than diminished. For three months Shabbathai held his court at Abydos, the centre of an admiring multitude, while the Jewish communities of the rest of Europe were riven into Sabbathaism and anti-Sabbathaism, for some Jews still retained their mental balance. The fundamental alterations in the Jewish ritual that Shabbathai had ordered had also shocked and opened the eyes of many who were once his adherents. His end came with his denunciation to the Sultan by a rival Jewish prophet. He was given the alternatives of death or Islam and chose the milder one. His apostasy was another shock to many of his followers whose number was thereby greatly reduced. But hosts still remained and followed him on his road to Islam arguing that even an assumed apostasy was a necessary preliminary to the fulfilment of his mission. These followers kept together as Crypto-Jews—heretics both in Judaism and in Islam—marrying only among themselves—and survive as the sect of Dönmeh until to-day. Nominal Moslems, they are still in essentials Jews, but their Judaism is polluted by the belief in Shabbathai as the Messiah who will return in due course to redeem the world and reconcile its inhabitants. As for Shabbathai himself, the Sultan accepted his adoption of Islam and gave him a subordinate office in his palace. Intrigues on his part led to his banishment. A source to some extent of further misfortunes to the Jews, he never recovered anything approaching his old position and he died in 1676, ten years after the date of his apotheosis, forgotten by most of his former worshippers, at Dulcigno.

CHAPTER III

THE BRITISH ATTITUDE

Jewish Settlement in Palestine: British Protection of the Jews: Shaftesbury: Palmerston: Finn: The Damascus Blood Accusation: Gawler's and other Projects: Laurence Oliphant: Edward Cazalet: Advocates of a Jewish State.

AFTER THE controversies that arose around the re-settlement of the Jews in England in the seventeenth century had subsided, apart from an occasional short-lived incursion of a Jewish question into prominence, the topic of the Jews did not become one of general interest until the end of the eighteenth century. This time it was closely linked with that of Palestine. A group of writers and pamphleteers, most prominent among whom was Joseph Priestley, the scientist and political thinker, suddenly came into existence with schemes for the re-settlement of the Jews in Palestine. James Bicheno, a dissenting minister and schoolmaster, was the most active of them. As early as 1800, he saw in the then almost universal war and a revolution in political ideas that can be compared only with that of Bolshevism a century and a quarter later, portents of the imminent restoration of the Jews to Palestine. He looked to one of the great powers as the instrument of that restoration and was fearful least Britain would let the opportunity pass into the hands of France. Bicheno found a vigorous opponent in Thomas Witherby, whose opposition lay for the most part in the direction of Church of England versus Dissent, for he also looked forward to the 'partial restoration of many of them (the Jews) to their own land', but through the instrumentality of the Protestant powers. The intervention of France, either Catholic or Atheist, was unthinkable.

Suspicion of France and of Napoleon was magnified if not created by the latter's coquetting not only with the Jews of France, who were in the early years of his period of power suffering from very heavy disabilities, but with those of the whole world. His invasion of Palestine had been marked by a manifesto addressed to the Jews of Asia and Africa promising the re-creation of a Jewish state, and when a few years later he convened a Jewish conference and later a 'Sanhredim' to regulate the relations between the Jews and the peoples among whom they dwelt, his invitations were sent to the Jews of all countries.

Bicheno, Witherby and the others were only private individuals who spoke for themselves or at the most for small circles of friends or sympathizers. British official interest arose in the year 1838 when the British Government established a consulate in Jerusalem, the first of the powers to do so, at any rate since the year 1583 when an English consul was also appointed to Jerusalem jointly with other towns in Syria. The British interests in Palestine were sufficient to justify the establishment of this consulate. The Jewish population of Palestine cannot therefore be taken as the reason for it, but its presence undoubtedly contributed towards the decision. Jewry and Palestine Jewry were already matters of interest in British governing circles and any doubt that might be raised must be dispersed at once by the instructions given by Palmerston to the newly-appointed vice-Consul in one of the earliest of his dispatches 'to afford protection to the Jews generally: and you will take an early opportunity of reporting . . . upon the present state of the Jewish population in Palestine.' This did not mean British Jews, for there were not a dozen in the country then. The incentive behind Palmerston and the Government was undoubtedly Lord Shaftesbury, then Lord Ashley, the philanthropist and pioneer of social service, who although a consistent opponent on religious grounds of the political emancipation of the Jews of Britain, was throughout a long life an ardent advocate of the welfare of the Jews of Palestine and of the settlement of other Jews there. In this he was influenced by both philanthropy and religion. The appointment of a British Consul to Jerusalem coincided with the publication of a volume of travels by Lord Lindsay, a scholar and widely read author, afterwards Lord Crawford and Balcarres, in which he displayed a very sympathetic attitude towards the idea of the restoration of the Jews to Palestine. This book and its references to the Jews attracted widespread attention which culminated in a two-column article in *The Times*, in which the Palestine proposals were recommended to the sympathetic consideration of its readers. Equal attention was gained by an article in the *Quarterly Review*, now known to have been written by Shaftesbury, in which he emphasized the coincidence of British and Jewish interests in the East and urged a still further measure of British protection for the Jews there. Shaftesbury, who was a family connexion of Palmerston's, frequently pressed his views regarding Palestine on the Foreign Minister and again it was in consequence of his representations that the British Ambassador in Constantinople was instructed in August 1840 to urge on the Turkish Government the advisability, in Turkish interests, of offering every possible encouragement to the Jews of Europe to return to Palestine. As a necessary preliminary to such a return, it was at the same time pointed out, an improvement in the political and civic situation of the Jews of the Ottoman Empire and the safeguarding of their rights were essential. Further representations on similar lines were made from time to time at Constantinople. The British Consul, once settled in Jerusalem, found the greater part of his time engaged in affording protection and advice to Jews of all nations and this continued for many years and at times led to difficulties with the Ottoman Government which as time passed resented, more and more, interference at any rate between itself and its own subjects. The second British Consul to be appointed, James Finn, who in the fervour of his Jewish sympathies frequently exceeded the instructions that were given him, after he had been in the country some years, formally put forward a plan 'to persuade Jews in a large body to settle there as agriculturists on the soil.' His proposal was in no sense political and in common with all sympathizers, contemporary and subsequent, with a practical knowledge of Palestine and its problems, he argued that 'in forming rural colonies the immigrants, with regard to their own advantage and the peace of the country, should be recommended and persuaded to do so in partnership with the Arab peasantry.' The Foreign Office was friendly to the suggestion and referred it to Constantinople but nothing came of it.

The foregoing are but a few selected references to

THE BRITISH ATTITUDE 31

British interest in the Jews and their connexion with Palestine, during the earlier half of the nineteenth century. Their number can be multiplied several times. *The Times* in particular opened its columns to consideration of the subject and was generous in the space it allotted to it. Shaftesbury was active in unofficial as well as official circles. He even went so far as to issue a questionnaire—it is not now known who were the subjects of his inquiries—in order to obtain material for the pursuit of his campaign. *The Times*[1] published particulars of this inquiry under the heading 'Syria—Restoration of the Jews (From a Correspondent).'

'The proposition to plant the Jewish people in the land of their fathers, under the protection of the five Powers, is no longer a mere matter of speculation, but of serious political consideration. In a ministerial paper of the 31st of July an article appears bearing all the characteristics of a feeler on this deeply interesting subject. However, it has been reserved for a noble lord opposed to Her Majesty's Ministers to take up the subject in a practical and statesman-like manner, and he is instituting enquiries, of which the following is a copy:—

QUERIES

"'1. What are the feelings of the Jews you meet with respect to their return to the Holy Land?
"'2. Would the Jews of station and property be inclined to return to Palestine, carry with them their capital, and invest it in the cultivation of the land, if by the operation of law and

The Times, 17 August, 1840.

justice, life and property were rendered secure?

"'3. How soon would they be inclined and ready to go back?

"'4. Would they go back entirely at their own expense, requiring nothing further than the assurance of safety to person and estate?

"'5. Would they be content to live under the Government of the country as they should find it, their rights and privileges being secured to them under the protection of the European Powers?

"'Let the answers you procure be as distinct and decided and detailed as possible: in respect as to the enquiries as to property, it will of course be sufficient that you should obtain fair proof of the fact from general report."

'The noble Lord who is instituting these enquiries has given deep attention to the matter, and is well known as the writer of an able article in the *Quarterly* on the subject, in December, 1838.'

A few months earlier, a memorandum[1] permeated with religious mysticism and replete with biblical references was addressed to the Governments of the Protestant states in Europe and America, 'Dictated by the peculiar conjuncture of affairs in the East, and the other striking "signs of the times",' it 'reverts to the original covenant which secures that land (Palestine) to the descendants of Abraham, and urges on the consideration of the powers addressed what may be the probable line of duty on the part of Protestant Christendom

[1] *The Times*, 26 August, 1840

THE BRITISH ATTITUDE

to the Jewish people in the present controversy in the East.' It called for a new Cyrus to rebuild the Temple in Jerusalem. Of a more practical character was a memorial presented to Palmerston in November 1840 by the Acting Committee of the General Assembly of the Church of Scotland for Promoting Christianity among the Jews. This followed on a mission of inquiry sent to Palestine by the General Assembly in the previous year. The Acting Committee looked forward to a deeper interest by Britain in Palestine. 'They are most anxious that, in any future settlement of that country, under the auspices of Britain, your Lordship and Her Majesty's Government should take measures, as far as possible, for protecting the Jews against oppression and injustice, to which recent events have shown that they are still liable."

Palmerston's dispatches of the year 1840 and Shaftesbury's intensified activities at that time were probably influenced by a *cause célébre*, the 'recent events' to which the General Assembly referred, which permeated the whole of Europe. On the 5th of February of that year Padre Tommaso, a Capuchin monk, well known in Damascus, disappeared. The members of his church, inspired by medieval superstitions and prejudices that had many a time brought massacre and destruction to Jewish communities, promptly accused the Jews of the city of having murdered him in order to obtain his blood for the approaching Passover. The Consul for France, who had the Latins of the East under his protection, at once intervened and took up the case of his protégés. He denounced the leading Jews of Damascus to the local authorities by whom they were imprisoned and tortured to force a confession. Some of them, men of position, died under their sufferings. The mob, encouraged by the behaviour of the authorities and with the tacit approval of the French, attacked the Jewish quarter, set fire to it and looted its contents. The Consul for France, hitherto the prosecutor, now took up the position of judge. Since the accusers were his protégés he was in a position to do so. He tried the accused and found all of them guilty not only of murdering Father Tommaso but also of having used his blood for ritual purposes. It was then left to the local authorities to hang the prisoners.

Syria was at the time under the control of Mehemet Ali, the Pasha of Egypt, who had revolted against his suzerain, the Sultan, and had invaded his Asiatic dominions. Mehemet's consent was necessary before the prisoners could be executed and the matter was referred to him in Alexandria. In the meanwhile the news had spread throughout Europe and aroused horror in every capital. In London at a Mansion House meeting the Blood Accusation was denounced and the sympathy of the people of London and of England offered to the Jews in their trials. Similar representative meetings were held in Paris and in North America. The Jews of England and France were also roused and sent their leading men, Sir Moses Montefiore from England, Adolph Crémieux, the statesman, from France, to Egypt to intercede with Mehemet Ali. Montefiore went after an interview at the Foreign Office and with the full support of Palmerston who promised every effort for the protection of the Jews of the East. In Alexandria the mission, which had also the support of the Austrian Government, was completely successful. The imprisoned Jews of Damascus were declared innocent and released and Mehemet went further and declared the Blood Accusation in general to be without basis. Montefiore returned to England through Constantinople where he received similar assurances from the Sultan who had in the meanwhile recovered control over Syria.

As the nineteenth century advanced British interest in Palestine and its Jewish relationship increased. Official interest was for the most part confidential, but it was none the less active in that account as the archives of the Foreign Office show. For unofficial interest there was no occasion for concealment and throughout the past century pamphleteer followed politician and politician pamphleteer in announcing his own panacea for the future of Palestine, and although these proposals were seldom in complete agreement they were unanimous in expressing sympathy with what were believed to be the desires of the Jews and their advantage. George Gawler, one-time Governor of South Australia, who claimed to be the virtual founder of that colony, published in 1845 a pamphlet in which he advocated the establishment of Jewish agricultural colonies in Palestine with local self-government and in external affairs under the control of the British Consul acting in consultation with the Turkish authorities. Incidentally he protested against the proposals of others, less realistic and more visionary. 'Wild schemes' he dubbed them, and they were certainly far less statesmanlike and reasonable than his own. The one centre point was however common to all of them, Gawler's and the others, Jewish agricultural settlement under British protection—a direct foreshadowing of the terms of the mandate of eighty years later. As for the financial side, Gawler said bluntly that this should be the care of the Christian nations in expiation for their treatment of the Jews in the past and in gratitude for all they owed to them. Gawler had a not unsympathetic reception, the *Spectator* being in the forefront of his supporters, a moderate and reasoned one. In particular the writer in that periodical emphasized that the only hope of a satisfactory settlement was in co-operation with the Ottoman Government. With Gawler a Jewish settlement in Palestine was not a passing interest. He continued over a period of some ten years to be active in endeavouring to translate his proposals into concrete measures. In another respect also he showed himself a forerunner of some non-Jewish Zionists who followed long after him. He saw in a prosperous self-supporting Jewish population in Palestine a British asset.

'Divine Providence has placed Syria and Egypt in the very gap between England and the most important regions of her colonial and foreign trade, India, China, the Indian Archipelago and Australia. She does not require and wish for increase of territory—already has she (that dangerous boon), more direct dominion than she can easily maintain, but she does *most urgently* need the shortest and the safest lines of communication to the territories already possessed. . . . Egypt and Syria stand in intimate connection. A foreign hostile power mighty in either, would soon endanger British trade and communications through the other. Hence the loud providential call upon her, to exert herself energetically for the amelioration of the condition of both of these provinces. Egypt has improved greatly by British influence, and it is now for England to set her hand to the renovation of Syria, through the only people whose energies will be

THE BRITISH ATTITUDE 37

extensively and permanently in the work—the real children of the soil, the sons of Israel.'[1]

While Gawler was working in England to convert people to his views, Finn, the British Consul and his wife, were doing practical work towards the same end in Jerusalem. There the problem was to provide for the relatively large Jewish pauper population, without occupation and practically without means of support. The Finns took the matter in hand, rented a piece of land and set unemployed Jews to work, building cisterns and growing food. This was in fact the initiation of the Jewish agricultural revival in Palestine which is now represented by thousands of acres of orange groves, fields of corn and of vegetables and fruit orchards, and scores of villages, some of them grown into small towns. The Finns, as their work developed, found it quite beyond their means and had to turn to friends in England for assistance. Thus was formed the Society for the Promotion of Jewish Agricultural Labour in the Holy Land, entirely under Christian auspices, which after one or two changes of name, continued its activities until the British Government under the Mandate had taken Jewish welfare in Palestine under its charge and the objects of the society having been fully attained, there was no further need for it. There were at least two other societies active towards the same end in Gawler's time. One was a joint English Jewish and Christian undertaking, the Association for Promoting Jewish Settlements in Palestine. The other, an American undertaking, was sponsored by Warder Cresson, an eccentric, who had been Consul for the United States

[1] *Syria and its near Prospects.*

in Jerusalem, had adopted Judaism and settled in the country.

Of all the British advocates of the settlement of Jews in Palestine the most interesting was undoubtedly the eccentric mystic and rolling stone, Laurence Oliphant. He first had his attention directed to Palestine and the Jews about the year 1879 when he visited the country, and later he went to Constantinople to obtain a concession of Northern Palestine with a view to the settlement of Jews there. This project had the benevolent sympathy of the British Government behind it and the encouragement of the Prince of Wales, later King Edward. For financial assistance Oliphant trusted to the visionaries of England and America, but he never put them to the test, for he obtained no success at the Porte. 'Any amount of money can be raised upon it,' he said, owing to the belief which people have that they would be fulfilling prophecy and bringing on the end of the world. 'I don't know why they are so anxious for this latter event,' he continued with a flash of wisdom, 'but it makes the commercial speculation easy.' This scheme of Oliphant's, apart from its Jewish aspects, looked towards the furtherance of British policy of resuscitating Turkey and binding it to the British connexion. Oliphant's project always contemplated a Jewish settlement, politically an integral part of the Ottoman Empire. Oliphant's real contribution to the Jewish re-settlement in Palestine was the assistance he rendered to the Roumanian immigrants who ultimately founded the village of Zichron Jacob. He was then living in Haifa where he had settled and remained for some years. The immigrants had come in the belief that land for the purchase of which they or their friends had provided

THE BRITISH ATTITUDE

the money had been acquired for them and, somewhat naïvely, that all that was necessary was to settle in their new homes. But when they reached Haifa they found that the situation was very different. There they were stranded, miles from their proposed home, a home very much in prospect, with their scanty means becoming rapidly exhausted, and starvation almost visible round the corner. Oliphant, hearing of them and their troubles, immediately came to their assistance. To some extent he supported them out of his own pocket. More important was the interest in them that he aroused in Baron Edmond de Rothschild of Paris, who took their affairs in hand, smoothed out all the difficulties in their way and ultimately settled them on the land they had left Roumania to cultivate. There they and their descendants have remained and Zichron Jacob, named in memory of Baron Edmond's father, is now a prosperous little village on the eve of celebrating its sixtieth birthday. Oliphant in interesting Rothschild in these Roumanian immigrants did far more than secure their future and that of their village. He introduced Rothschild to Jewish settlement in Palestine in furtherance of which he subsequently devoted a great fortune, and on lines that, while benefiting the new settlers, threatened the interests of no one else. One consequence was that in later times when Palestine was the centre of upheaval, with the Arabs seething with fear and hatred of the Jewish newcomers, peace was seldom disturbed on the Rothschild lands where Jews and Arabs had for a generation learnt to dwell together in amity.

Oliphant gave a picturesque account of the negotiations that led to the acquisition of the land on which the village is built.

'The meeting took place in the storehouse, where Jews and Arabs squatted promiscuously amid the heaps of grain, and chaffered over the terms of their mutual co-partnership. It would be difficult to imagine anything more utterly incongruous than the spectacle thus presented—the stalwart fellahin, with their wild, shaggy, black beards, the brass hilts of their pistols projecting from their waistbands, their tasselled kufeihahs drawn tightly over their heads and girdled with coarse black cords, their loose, flowing abbas, and sturdy bare legs and feet: and the ringleted, effeminate-looking Jews, in Caftans reaching almost to their ankles, as oily as their red or sandy locks, or the expression of the countenances—the former inured to hard labour on the burning hill-sides of Palestine, the latter fresh from the Ghetto of some Roumanian town, unaccustomed to any other description of exercise than that of their wits, but already quite convinced that they knew more about agriculture than the people of the country, full of suspicion of all advice tendered to them, and animated by a pleasing self-confidence which I fear the first practical experience will rudely belie. In strange contrast with these Roumanian Jews was the Arab Jew who acted as interpreter—a stout, handsome man, in oriental garb, as unlike his European co-religionists as the fellahin themselves. My friend and myself, in the ordinary costume of the British or American tourist, completed the party.

'The discussion was protracted beyond midnight—the native peasants screaming in Arabic, the Roumanian Israelites endeavouring to out-talk them in German jargon, the interpreter vainly trying to make himself heard, everybody at cross-purposes because no one was patient enough to listen till another had finished, or modest enough to wish to hear anybody speak but himself. Tired out, I curled myself on an Arab coverlet, which seemed principally stuffed with fleas, but sought repose in vain. At last a final rupture was arrived at, and the fellahin left us, quivering with indignation at the terms proposed by the newcomers. Sleep brought better counsel to both sides, and an arrangement was finally arrived at next morning which I am afraid has only to be put into operation to fail signally."

A contemporary of Oliphant's was Edward Cazalet, a British industrialist with considerable interest in Russia, where he had come in contact with the Jewish population of the Pale of Settlement, the sufferings of whom had aroused his sympathies. He also saw a coincidence of Jewish and British interests in Palestine—the peace and prosperity of a region lying athwart British communications with her Empire—and the need for affording the oppressed Jews of Eastern Europe an opportunity for regeneration under conditions very different from those to which they were accustomed. He went so far as to advocate a British protectorate of Palestine so that the interests of the Jewish population, to the growth of which he looked forward, would be thoroughly safeguarded. He was in other respects almost prophetic. He envisaged a railway to the Euphrates, a Baghdad Railway, both for economic and perhaps strategic reasons and also to provide employment at the beginning for the thousands of Jewish immigrants who he expected would settle in Palestine. He also advocated the establishment of a

Jewish university in Palestine, a project that was among the first to be fulfilled after the British occupation of the country. His proposals came to naught, partly in consequence of the suspicion with which every British proposal was viewed at the Porte after the accession to power in 1880 of Gladstone. Cazalet, who had some influential support in England, afterwards considerably modified his scheme, abandoning the suggestion of a British protectorate and not tying himself down to Palestine, but offering to accept any suitable region in the Ottoman dominions. But the Porte would still have none of it. It is interesting to note as an instance of heredity, reinforced perhaps by environment, that Edward Cazalet's grandson to-day is as enthusiastic and active in forwarding Jewish wishes in Palestine as was his grandfather sixty years ago.

Oliphant and Cazalet did not stand alone. They have been selected for detailed mention since they attracted most attention. A number of other English public men between the time of Gawler and that of Oliphant pointed in the same direction. Prominent among them was the group that centred in the Palestine Exploration Fund, a purely scientific, non-political and unsectarian society, many of whose active members could, however, not avoid the attraction that the Jewish question and its connexion with Palestine exercise over many minds. Outstanding in this group is Claude Conder, who in the later decades of his life devoted a great part of his energies to furthering the cause of Jewish settlement in Palestine with the beginnings of which his frequent visits to the country had made him well acquainted.

There was one element common to all of the foregoing projects and also to others which have passed without mention. That was that none of them envisaged anything of the nature of a Jewish state in a political sense. They all, or most of them, proposed a measure of local autonomy, of municipal and even of communal self-government, but that was all. Politically Palestine, no matter how large the Jewish population was to become, was to remain a part of a larger state, the Ottoman Empire as a rule, even in those cases in which Britain was to be given a special status as protector. A smaller group of British enthusiasts was, however, less far-seeing, enthusiastic, over-enthusiastic in its zeal for the furtherance of Jewish interests, so enthusiastic as to risk imperilling them. One of the first of these advocates of political Zionism, far in advance of any modern Jewish advocate of such a policy was Colonel Charles Henry Churchill. Having settled in Syria he knew the country well and had come to the conclusion that a diligent self-supporting Jewish population would bring benefit both to itself and to the country. His plan was, put baldly, the reconstitution of the Jewish kingdom. With his plans more or less developed he went to Sir Moses Montefiore, who was not only the head of the British Jewish community but a man who had shown much practical as well as sentimental interest in the settlement of Jews in Palestine. But a Jewish kingdom formed no part of his plan and Churchill obtained no encouragement from him. The result of the interview was a considerable cooling of Churchill's enthusiasm. However, so far as he was interested in the welfare of the Jews of Palestine he was encouraged and Montefiore entrusted him with funds for the relief of distress there among all classes of the population.

Churchill did not stand alone nor did the discouragement

he had received from Anglo-Jewry deter his fellow dreamers, if they were aware of it. He had barely retired from the scene when a Church of England clergyman, Thomas Tully Crybbace, came forward with a similar proposal. He proposed to form an international society 'for the restoration of the Jewish Nation to Palestine', held meetings in furtherance of his object, published pamphlets and appealed to the Queen and Parliament for support. His inspiration was largely biblical and religious, but it was also to some extent political. A Jewish Palestine was to his mind a British interest in view of the road to India. He therefore urged that the British Government should call on the Porte to surrender the whole land 'from the Euphrates to the Nile, and from the Mediterranean to the Desert' and on the Czar to release his oppressed Jewish subjects. It would be the privilege of Britain to bring the land and people together and help both to flourish under its protection. Another advocate of a similar project, also a clergyman, was Samuel Alexander Bradshaw who, pointing out the responsibility of the Christian states in the matter, called on Parliament to vote four millions and the churches to grant a further million to provide means for the attainment of his object. Bradshaw, although he met with little or no response, nursed his project, for forty years later, in 1884, he was still advocating the restoration of the Jews to the Holy Land, as a nation, with Palestine as a British protectorate. This time he expected twenty millionaires to come forward and subscribe half a million each and thus make their peace with heaven. A third advocate of the 're-establishment of the Jewish nation in Palestine, under British protection,' in the middle 'forties, was E. L. Mitford, a

THE BRITISH ATTITUDE

Ceylon civil servant. He put forward a further argument that the growth of population in Palestine would relieve the depression of the manufacturers of Manchester, Birmingham and Glasgow. He also looked forward ultimately to a fully independent Jewish Palestinian state.

Sixteen years later, when the disturbance caused by the Crimean War had subsided, a new group of advocates of a Jewish state in Palestine arose. Thomas Clarke, a doctor of medicine, argued that the British and the Jews were natural allies, that the control of Palestine was essential to British interests and that that control could be secured only through a protectorate over a Jewish population. Ten years later Isaac Ashe, using the Anglo-Jewish Press as his vehicle, with an eye also on British interests in India and in the road thither, urged co-operation with the Ottoman Government with a view to the development 'of a national population sufficiently numerous and sufficiently free-spirited and self-reliant to be able to assert, in due time, national independence and self-government according to the representative institutions of England'. There was yet another group of advocates twenty years later, after Oliphant and Cazalet had withdrawn their more reasonable proposals, of a Jewish state under British protection or under the joint protection of the Powers, consisting again of clerics, and it was to this group that Bradshaw attached himself.

CHAPTER IV

PRACTICAL ZIONISM

Joseph Nasi and the Settlement of Tiberias: Montefiore and Jewish Settlement: Charles Netter: Abraham Benisch: Warder Cresson: Little Incentive to Emigrate: The Russian Persecution: The Lovers of Zion: The New Settlement: Edmond de Rothschild: Ahad Ha'Am.

PALESTINE HAS never been without Jewish inhabitants, not even after the suppression of the Bar Cochba rebellion when Jerusalem was laid waste, its name changed and Jews forbidden to approach within many miles, nor during the period of the Latin Kingdom, which was inaugurated by a bath of blood, Jews and Moslems being, wherever found, driven into their houses of worship and massacred among the burning ruins. In the earlier years that followed the final Roman conquest, Jews were probably more numerous in the villages than in the towns. As far as is known there was never any prohibition by the Romans on Jews engaging in agriculture, and this must at first have been their main occupation. In the towns they were more obvious and more likely to attract the unwelcome attention of their rulers. In the towns also the opportunities for an impoverished population to maintain itself were less. Thus violence, poverty and migration, all con-

PRACTICAL ZIONISM

tinued to reduce the number of the Jews in the towns and to swell the Jewish rural population. In the course of centuries the tide turned. Life, unguarded in the villages, for Jews still more than for the other sections of the population, generally known as Arab not so much on account of their origins as of their language, was too dangerous to continue. The Jewish agriculturists gradually disappeared, mostly it is probable by absorption in the surrounding population which already had many Judaean and Israelite elements. Others took refuge in the towns and newcomers, for only for brief periods was there no immigration of Jews into Palestine, themselves town dwellers, settled at once in the towns, in the "Holy Cities," the object of their pilgrimage. The Jews who settled in Palestine in the Middle Ages and in modern times, almost until the end of the nineteenth century, were, practically without exception, pilgrims, men whose whole lives were absorbed by their religious duties and exercises, who came to Palestine to study, to pray, to die, without thought of anything else.

Of this earlier Jewish agricultural population there is one curious survival in a group of Jews, indistinguishable from their Arab neighbours, in the little village of Pekiin or Bukeah in Northern Galilee. The origin of this group is unknown either to its members, its neighbours or the other Jews of Palestine. It goes back before the memory of man. In all respects but one these villagers live, work and look like their neighbours. They are agriculturists and artizans and, also like their neighbours, terribly poor. The one difference is that they are Jews by religion, living in a Moslem setting. This little remnant was re-discovered, so far as the Western World is concerned, by Andrew Bonar and Robert Murray M'Cheyne, two Scottish divines who visited the country to investigate the condition of the Jews in 1838. Sir Moses Montefiore who was there in the following year, was the first Western Jew to learn of their existence. Thirty-eight years later Lord, then Lieutenant, Kitchener, while working on the survey of Palestine, discovered them again. He expressed the opinion that the Jews of Pekiin were then the only ones in Palestine still owning and tilling land and remarked on the number of ruins of ancient synagogues in their neighbourhood. The earliest known reference to the Jews of Pekiin is in 1522.

The earliest practical project for the settlement of foreign Jews in Palestine was that of Joseph Nasi, Duke of Naxos. This interesting personage was one of the many Jewish refugees from the Inquisition in Portugal. He fled first to Antwerp and later to Venice and Turkey. A member of a distinguished and wealthy family, he quickly acquired a position of consequence in his new home. The Sultan, knowing of him by repute, at once turned to him for advice. He became influential at court, had titles and honours conferred on him, and after the Pretender Bayazid had been defeated and driven into exile, the Sultan Selim, in recognition of Nasi's services—he always described him as 'a model of the Princes of the Jewish Nation'—gave him a grant of Tiberias and the neighbouring villages where he might carry out his project for Jewish settlement. Nasi set about the task of rebuilding the city. He planted mulberry trees for the breeding of silkworms, took steps for the production of wool and the manufacture of cloth and invited the Jews of Europe and especially those of the Papal States, whose position had recently become precarious, to settle on the lands of his concession. Some hundreds of Italian Jews left their homes in response to the invitation, some of whom at any rate never reached their destination, being waylaid by pirates and sold into slavery. The story of this venture of Nasi's is, however, involved in obscurity. That nothing came of it is certain: the causes of the failure are, however, unknown.

It was not far from Pekiin, in the neighbourhood of Safad, that Montefiore on his visit to Palestine in 1839 proposed to set up Jewish agricultural settlements. He described his plan in his diary. 'I shall apply to Mohamed Ali for a grant of land for fifty years; some one or two hundred villages; giving him an increased rent of from ten to twenty per cent., and paying the whole in money annually at Alexandria, but the land and villages to be free, during the whole term, from every tax or rate either of Pasha or governor of the several districts; and liberty being accorded to dispose of the produce in any quarter of the globe. The grant obtained, I shall, please Heaven, on my return to England, form a company for the cultivation of the land and the encouragement of our brethren in Europe to return to Palestine. . . . By degrees I hope to induce the return of thousands of our brethren to the Land of Israel. I am sure they would be happy in the enjoyment of the observance of our holy religion, in a manner which is impossible in Europe.' Mehemet Ali was not unsympathetic and Montefiore's scheme might have been realized, but Palestine almost immediately passed out of his control, and no proposals regarding that country any longer concerned him. Montefiore's interest in the settlement of Jews in Palestine, however, did not lapse with the failure of this project. He paid a number of visits to the country, on every occasion showing an active interest in the welfare of its population and contributing generously towards relieving their needs. Outside of Jerusalem he built almshouses, towards which a legacy bequeathed to him as trustee by an American Jewish philanthropist helped, for the use of the Jewish poor of the City. He founded the first school for Jewish girls in Palestine, and, with British Government support, secured permission for the building of a synagogue for the Ashkenazi Jews. At the same time he did not forget his ideal of a Jewish agricultural population. As a beginning he purchased some land near Jaffa on which he established two or three Jewish families with every encouragement and assistance to establish themselves permanently. Circumstances were, however, against him. His expectations were not realized and after some difficulties and a certain amount of annoyance the Montefiore land was ultimately absorbed into the Jewish town of Tel Aviv, the possibility of whose existence in Montefiore's time was inconceivable. Another failure of his in regard to Palestine, to be made good by others after his death, was a project for a railway connexion of Jaffa and Jerusalem. In this also he was in advance of his time. Montefiore paid his last visit to Palestine when in his ninety-first year, on this occasion also going on a philanthropic mission to investigate the position of the

Jews there and to gather material on which to base schemes for its improvement.

Montefiore lived until 1885, dying in his hundred and first year, but living long enough to see the beginning of the realization of his dreams, the first steps in an agricultural and industrial development which has culminated in a Jewish population comprising a third of the total population of to-day and differing from the Palestine Jewry of Montefiore's time in that it consists overwhelmingly of modern European men and women, pulsating with all the interests and activities of the West. Although the most prominent in his lifetime of the Jewish advocates of the regeneration of Palestine and of the Jewish people there, he was by no means the only one. There were even a few practical experiments, none of which however proved permanent, although the first settlement of Petach Tikva, now, after Tel Aviv the largest all-Jewish town in Palestine, was made as an agricultural village in 1878. It was abandoned after a brief existence. One project, initiated by George Gawler, who formed the Palestine Society, afterwards the Palestine Colonization Fund, in which both Jews and Christians co-operated for its furtherance, succeeded in interesting the Turkish Government who promised those Jewish settlers who would become Ottoman subjects free grants of land and exemption from taxation for twelve years, with local and communal autonomy. But settlers were not forthcoming.

The great event of this period was the establishment, in 1870, of a Jewish agricultural school, Mikveh Israel, near Jaffa. The land on which the school was built was presented by the Turkish Government. The idea came from Hirsch Kalischer and Elijah Gutmacher German rabbis, but the practical initiative from Charles Netter, a prominent French Jew who had helped to found ten years earlier the *Alliance Israèlite Universelle* to watch over the interests of Jews in the backward countries and to provide them with opportunities for education. Mikveh Israel was, until many years later it became self-supporting, assisted and directed by the *Alliance Israèlite* which also supported and still supports a number of Jewish schools in Palestine.

There was one other project for Jewish settlement in Palestine which deserves special mention. Its projector although not British by birth was British by adoption. Abraham Benisch was born in Bohemia and educated in Vienna. While at the university he and other Jewish students developed an interest in Palestine and the Jewish future there. They formed a small students' society to secure the settlement of Jews in the Holy Land and Benisch was sent abroad to obtain support for their proposals, in other Jewish communities. He came to England in 1841, but got little sympathy among the Jews there. However he secured some interest in Government circles and at the instance of Lord Canning, the Under Secretary for Foreign Affairs, submitted to him a memorandum advocating British protection of the Jews of Palestine and under that protection the establishment of agricultural and commercial settlements of Jews in that country, Benisch did not suggest that these should be outside of the jurisdiction of the Ottoman Government, but that Britain should keep an eye on their welfare and their rights. In fact he wanted only that these projected settlements, which meant a much larger Jewish population and probably more problems, should receive the same protection and encouragement as Britain was giving and was about to give through its representative in Jerusalem to the existing Jewish population. The extension of British official interest in the welfare of the Jews of Palestine was perhaps an outcome of this memorandum. Benisch settled in London. He very quickly shed the political tinge of his original proposals but he never lost his interest in the welfare of the Jews of Palestine. Some thirty years later he helped to found the Anglo-Jewish Association which still concerns itself with the education of Palestine Jewry. Eighteen years earlier he was the principal founder of the joint Jewish-Christian Association for Promoting Jewish Settlements in Palestine, whose objects were a concession of derelict land in the neighbourhood of Tiberias and Safad on which to settle Jews, the settlements to enjoy local autonomy, and to obtain support in England for the assistance of these settlements until they could stand on their own feet. It was this Association, which afterwards developed into the Palestine Colonization Fund, which secured considerable encouragement from the Turkish Minister in London, but like all its predecessors and contemporaries there was no practical result.

Another projector of Jewish agricultural settlement in Palestine, who may be counted as a Jew or a Christian as one feels inclined, was Warder Cresson, an American quaker who was appointed the first United States consul in Jerusalem in 1844. He had previously come under Jewish influence and had shown tendencies in the direction of adopting the Jewish faith. He ultimately took this step, after he had been four years in the Holy Land, discarding his own name and taking that of Michael Boaz Israel. In America there was an attempt by his family to have him declared insane but this failed. On his return to Palestine he devoted his interest and money to the agricultural regeneration of the country and its Jewish inhabitants. He took steps to settle Jews on the land near Jerusalem and appealed to the American and European Jewish publics for assistance not only in this project but also in other similar ones in which Jews from Europe were to be invited to participate. However his proposals met with the same fate as the others. They died from lack of interest elsewhere.

Thus projects for the creation of self-supporting agricultural settlements of Jews in Palestine had followed one another almost continuously for the greater part of a century, but without exception they had all failed. Most of them had never reached the point of attempted realization: they were still-born. They were unable to arouse any enthusiasm, hardly any interest, except in a few individuals. The time was not yet ripe. There were men in Palestine who were attracted by the idea of supporting themselves on the land: there were Jews and Christians elsewhere who somewhat tepidly would have liked to encourage them to do so. There were also Jews and Christians who for one reason or another would have liked to see a movement of Jews from Europe to Palestine. The religious incentive, not very strong among those out of whom agriculturists could have been made, existed. There was the economic one also, among the philanthropists, even if the prospective

PRACTICAL ZIONISM 55

settlers were for the most part inclined to follow the line of least resistance and remain where they were. In those days as in the present time the great masses of Jewry were by no means prosperous. Very large numbers were never far from destitution. But they lived their own lives, for the most part uninterfered with. It is true that in the whole of Eastern Europe they were excluded from the larger life of the country as well as from many callings, but few of them had any desire for that larger life. In Western Europe where Jews were the equals of their fellow-citizens, or as in Germany under few disabilities, there was little desire to emigrate and none to go to a country with a lower standard of civilization. Among the liberals who had left Central Europe in the reaction that had followed the abortive revolutions of 1848 there were many Jews, and many of the most valuable additions to the commercial, industrial and scientific life of England, France and America that have enriched those countries during the past century, were direct consequences of the political failures of 1848. These helped to build up the Jewries of those countries. To an equal if not a greater extent they benefited those countries as a whole. Settlement in Palestine, in any capacity, can never have crossed the minds of any of these exiles. They wanted a larger, not a smaller, life.

The change came in 1881. The murder of the Czar Alexander II in that year was followed by an outbreak of anti-Jewish outrages, in some cases massacres, in the Russian dominions, which were connived at, where not encouraged, by the authorities. The following year a series of repressive measures, nominally temporary, known collectively as the May Laws, was put in force. The natural consequence was the beginning of an exodus of the Jews from Russia. During the twenty years and longer in which this exodus proceeded some hundreds of thousands of Jews left Russia, for the most part for Britain and North America whose Jewish population was thereby increased manifold. A dribble of this exodus made its way to Palestine. Of this dribble a large portion turned to agriculture and by these settlers were dug the foundations of the present *Yishub*, the Jewish revival. A great part of the direction, the encouragement, the assistance of this new settlement in its beginning came from the *Choveve Zion*, the Lovers of Zion, an organization which, if not formally, was indirectly founded by Kalischer and Gutmacher, the German rabbis, Judah Alkalay, their colleague in Croatia, and Moses Hess, the pioneer German socialist, in the middle of the nineteenth century. Hitherto the idea had been mainly academic, but with the new movement towards Palestine it took concrete shape. *Choveve Zion* societies were founded in Russia, Roumania and Austria, and later in other countries. They included both prospective emigrants and also sympathizers with and encouragers of the emigration, the definite purpose being the assistance of the former class to secure their aim.

In Anglo-Jewry the movement obtained considerable encouragement and had the open support of many of its most prominent men. Among the Jews of England there had always been some sympathy, even though an inactive one, as has been indicated in earlier pages, with projects for the rehabilitation of the Jews in Palestine and when practical measures were proposed

PRACTICAL ZIONISM

with some promise of success, this sympathy was aroused from its sleep. Palestine also offered some measure of relief, albeit a very small one, for the miseries of the Jews of Eastern Europe. In the new era when a land of refuge for the exiles from Russia was urgent, settlement in Palestine took on a new complexion.

Three settlements sprang up almost simultaneously in the summer and autumn of 1882. The first of these, Rishon le-Zion (The First in Zion), was planted on the plain inland a few miles from Jaffa. Of the others Zichron Jacob, near Haifa, has already been mentioned in connexion with Laurence Oliphant. The third was in the hills of Galilee, Rosh Pina (The Cornerstone). The settlers were men of the towns who had previously hardly seen the country and its harvests, professional men, students, to a less extent shopkeepers and artizans. Their zeal they hoped would compensate for the absence of experience and knowledge. If this had been possible their success would have been assured, for their zeal was unbounded. But enthusiasm and devotion are not alone sufficient to make a doctor of medicine or philosophy a successful farmer or agricultural labourer. It is probable that all would have counted for nought if a generous and far-seeing patron had not appeared in the person of Baron Edmond de Rothschild. His introduction to Jewish settlement in Palestine at this time by Laurence Oliphant has already been mentioned. From that day to the last of his life fifty-two years later his devotion never flagged nor was his hand closed. Without him the new settlement movement would never have come to fruition, for zeal and energy are not enough. The settlements had to be given a fair chance of success from the very beginning and material assistance in their first years. For these purposes money was required, but the resources of the *Chovevé Zion* were very narrow. Rothschild, the millionaire, gave of his millions in furtherance of the new settlement. Many were the mistakes made by his agents, but he and they learnt from them and never hesitated to change a line of activity that did not seem to be meeting with success. From the assistance of others Rothschild passed to the establishment of settlements of his own. From agriculture also he passed to industry, building and financing factories and mills when he thought the demand for them existed, devoting the profits, if any, to the welfare of the workers or to the expansion of the settlement. He lived to see many of the settlements he had assisted or founded flourishing and firmly established. Everywhere in the Rothschild colonies and on Rothschild land Jews and Arabs lived side by side in friendship. There were no Arab grievances against Rothschild or his settlers and even in the worst periods of disturbance the Rothschild colonies as a rule remained outside the storm. Rothschild recognized that the overriding interest of the Jews of Palestine was the confidence and friendship of their Arab neighbours. The interests of the Arab cultivators of the land he bought were never overlooked, but by development he made this land capable of maintaining a population ten times its former size. Only the surplus was given to Jewish occupation. His work did not die with him. Many years before his death he transferred the management of his Palestine interests to the Jewish Colonization Association, the great organization for the education and training of the Jews of Eastern Europe, their employment in agriculture, and the settlement of some of them elsewhere, recognizing that the Association's experience and skill were and must be far greater than those of any organization he could create. Later a special organization, an offshoot of the Ica as it is known for short, was created in the Palestine Jewish Colonization Association, whose very valuable work continues under the chairmanship of his son, Mr. James de Rothschild, who has made England his home.

Rishon le-Zion, Zichron Jacob and Rosh Pina were the first of the new settlements. Rishon le-Zion in the midst of the orange country, is now a prosperous little town, the others large villages. Other settlements that Rothschild assisted in those early days were Petach Tikva, a revival of the failure of 1878, now a town, and Hedera, another prosperous and growing settlement. Rothschild's own settlements, Metullah and Ekron, were not so successful and have remained small. They did not have the advantage of orange-growing, the source of most if not all of the agricultural wealth of Palestine. But Benjamina and Pardes Anna, later Rothschild colonies, have flourished. The Ottoman Government was very tolerant in matters of self-government, especially where the Jewish population was concerned. All it required was its taxes and it was quite willing to accept them through an intermediary so long as they were forthcoming. In return it gave very little and did not interfere even in cases of petty crime so long as members of other communities were not affected. Thus these Jewish settlements enjoyed a wide measure of self-government, collecting the taxes and paying them

PALESTINE: A POLICY

to the Government from whom they heard nothing until the next pay-day arrived.

Baron Edmond de Rothschild and the *Chovevé Zion* were not the only organizations that established Jewish agricultural settlements in Palestine before the outbreak of war in 1914. But they were the principal ones. Even the Ica whose real interests were in Russia and North and South America, influenced by the settlements they were managing, established half a dozen small ones of their own in Galilee. There were also the *Bilu*, a group of Russian Jewish students, who were the first to cultivate Katrah, the Ezra Society of Berlin, the Independent Order B'nai B'rith, a Jewish friendly order especially strong in Germany and the United States of America, and others. Artuf was originally established by a missionary society for baptized Jews—Christian Israelites—who however failed. Artuf was later revived by a group of Bulgarian Jews. Others owe their existence to groups of private individuals and to rich philanthropists. The Zionist Organisation also began its colonization work before the outbreak of the war of 1914, but the results were still very meagre—Hulda not far from Lydda in the Sharon, Dagania on the Sea of Galilee.

The *Chovevé Zion* movement's title to a niche in Jewish history is that it marked the last stage in the preliminaries to the revival of Palestine by Jewish hands. It was the connecting link between the academic and theoretical Zionists of the past and the practical Zionists of the present, the life-line that rescued the earlier apparent failures and by attaching them to the present turned their failure into success. It had one

PRACTICAL ZIONISM 61

other title to fame. The *Chovevé Zion* was the passage through which Asher Ginzberg, better known by his pen-name, Ahad Ha'Am (One of the People), entered Jewish public life. Few would question that Ginzberg was the greatest and clearest thinker that Jewry has produced for Jewry in the last century. In his development he followed, up to a point, almost the normal course for a Russian Jew. A member of a Chassidic (the mystical and emotional school of Judaism) family, he studied from early childhood in the regular Talmudic schools. In their branch of Jewish scholarship he became an adept. He however passed beyond the limits of rabbinical scholarship, reached out to the wider modern learning, attended European universities and developed a critical mind. Later he became the modern philosopher of Judaism and the foremost stylist in modern Hebrew. He was first interested in the *Chovevé Zion* movement in 1884 and soon became one of its guiding members. In that organization he emphasized what have been termed the spiritual aspects of Zionism, throwing the emphasis on Jewish culture, the Jewish civilization, even before the more material Zionism, standing far away from any political tendencies the Movement might have. Quoting the obituary notice in *The Times*: 'Mr. Ginzberg gradually transferred its (the Zionist) centre of interest towards the conception of a Jewish nucleus in Palestine, where, undistracted by Gentile rivalries and beguilements, the Jews might create a purely Hebrew centre and civilization based on the Hebrew language and Hebrew literature, art and science. Such centre would serve as an inspiration for Jews elsewhere by forming a cultural rallying-

PALESTINE: A POLICY

point as a preservative against the disintegrating consequences of assimilation'.[1] After a few years' experience of the *Chovevé Zion* Ginzberg came to the conclusion that it did not completely fulfil the objects it had in view. It was immersing itself in colonization, in its devotion to the body of Jewry was forgetting its soul. To counteract this he formed within the *Chovevé Zion*, the *Bene Moshe* or Sons of Moses, intended to be future leaders of the Palestinian Movement, a mutual inspiration to one another, with the purpose ultimately of 'infusing their spirit into the people at large, and in

[1] Quoting Nahum Sokolow, than whom no one was better qualified to interpret Ahad Ha'Am, ' The revival of the Hebraic spirit does not depend upon the establishment of a certain number of colonies, but upon the establishment of a Jewish spiritual life in Palestine. Even a small settlement of Jews, not necessarily independent in the political sense but free from the cramping conditions of the Ghetto and made to draw its spiritual inspirations from Hebrew sources of the native soil, would breathe into the dead bones of Israel scattered in the Diaspora a Hebraic spirit; without which regeneration the Diaspora can have no hope to resist the overwhelming forces of assimilation. . . . The idea of a Hebrew culture must precede the restoration, in order to make Palestine Hebraic. . . . Only where the goal of our most cherished aspirations lies since we left for the long Exile can we begin a new life to carry out the ideas of the prophets. There only can the Hebrew spirit find a body, become a force in the life of Israel and effect a great moral influence even upon the emancipated Jews of Western Europe.' To Ahad Ha'Am the soul of Jewry was of far more consequence than its body, but he realized that a soul cannot live on earth without a body. Therefore a Jewish population in Palestine, a healthy, in mind and body, self-supporting Jewish population was a necessity, and one of some proportions relative to the total population of the country, but this did not mean that a Jewish majority in Palestine was a necessity, still less a Jewish state or government or army or navy. His ideal was a Palestinian state in which Jews might or might not form a majority but whose Jewish citizens would in all respects be free, the equals of the other citizens of the country, and in which Palestinian Jewry would also be free to develop its own culture, its own civilization, unimpeded by any outside force. To Ahad Ha'Am a Hebrew University in Jerusalem meant far more than a Hebrew post office or a Hebrew police force. (Ahad Ha'Am in using the term Hebrew referred to the race. For the religion he employed the word Judaism.)

restoring those moral qualities to it without which a people cannot exist as such'. Their influence was not direct and obvious. Nevertheless it was not ineffective. Quietly and barely perceptibly it worked and the direction given by Ahad Ha'Am and the *Bene Moshe* can be traced in many of the subsequent activities of the *Chovevé Zion*. Ultimately the *Chovevé Zion* became absorbed into the new Zionist Movement founded by Herzl, but not without a struggle. Ahad Ha'Am attended the first Zionist Congress in 1897 and found himself in disagreement with almost all of the views expressed by Herzl. He passed out of activity and devoted himself almost entirely to literature, but his disciples gained control of the Zionist Organisation in the end and he then came back as their mentor and adviser.

CHAPTER V

POLITICAL ZIONISM

Theodor Herzl: The New Zionism: The Basle Programme: El Arish and East Africa: Herzl's Successors: The Ito Secession.

THEODOR HERZL was a Viennese Jew, a typical son of Vienna or perhaps more properly of that cultured, lighthearted, friendly circle which gave pre-War Vienna its reputation and made it so attractive a city. Herzl was a Jew by birth—an Israelite in the sense used in the first chapter—as were so many of the other sons of the city, natural-born or adopted, as Herzl himself was; but the spirit of Vienna exorcised all other spirits and Herzl and the other members of the circle were neither Jew nor Christian nor even Austrian. They were Viennese. Herzl was, short of baptism, completely assimilated, one on whom his Judaism, his Jewish origin, lay so lightly, that it is probable that at this period of his life he often completely forgot it and when he did not do so he felt it so little as hardly to be affected. To these Viennese *par excellence* writing was almost as the breath of life; journalists, poets, novelists or dramatists were they all and Herzl was of course no exception. His father wanted him to be a lawyer, but this was out of the question. Journalism was his choice and from journalism he quickly developed into the feuilletonist, a natural child of such cities as Vienna and

Paris. Herzl however continued also as journalist in the more orthodox sense.

The course of his professional duties, as correspondent of the *Neue Freie Presse*, took Herzl to Paris. While there it was further his duty to write articles for his paper on the Dreyfus drama as it unfolded itself from day to day. Alfred Dreyfus, an almost completely assimilated Jew and zealous French officer, had been charged with treason. Probably the charge was originally made in good faith, a consequence of the lack of intelligence, reinforced perhaps by prejudice of those who made it. Prejudice, however, quickly gained the upper hand. The French Army, and in particular the War Office, was at that time a stronghold of reaction and of reaction Anti-Semitism is always a part. Those concerned who were not influenced by Anti-Jewish prejudice, if there were any, were as strongly influenced by another prejudice, that the army cannot be wrong and that a course once adopted must be pursued, without turning aside or hesitation, to its appointed end. Dreyfus had been accused by the War Office of treason. Therefore he was guilty. Any evidence or argument against that thesis was irrelevant, was almost itself treason. To the army Dreyfus's conviction was a matter of honour, to the Anti-Semites of France one of faith. It was in this milieu, one of whose possibility Herzl had never previously been conscious that he suddenly found himself.

The Dreyfus affair, the bitterness and hatred it aroused, had a remarkable effect on Herzl. It converted him to Judaism, or rather Hebraism, brought him back to the bosom of Jewry. He was no longer only an Israelite.

Herzl discovered, what he had forgotten, that he was a Jew; a Jew not in the selfish sense, but one with responsibilities to his fellow Jews. The Jewish question, the present and future of the Jews of the world, suddenly became a living one to him. The whole of his past dropped away. He saw only the Dreyfus Affair and the hatred and prejudice that boiled around it. Assimilation which had been a part of his being was suddenly proclaimed a hopeless failure. A Jew might be a Frenchman or a German or an Austrian but he was also a Jew, perhaps above all a Jew. The solution of the Jewish Question lay only in recognizing the Jews as a people and in bringing them together as one. A people cannot live without a country. Turning back to the definitions given in the first chapter, to be a Jew was of relatively little consequence, one must be a Hebrew. The first task therefore was the securing of a land which by means of its population, to be brought there, would be a Jewish or Hebrew one. At this time Herzl was not yet a Zionist, even though he had become a Jewish nationalist. He wanted a Jewish state. He did not rule out Palestine, but Palestine was not essential. His state could be formed in any land that was suitable and available. In this view he followed the example of others who had trodden the same path—Hess and Pinsker for instance. But like them he soon discovered that if his project were to be realized it could be only in Palestine. Elsewhere the spur—historic or sentimental or religious—without which a Jewish national state was unattainable was lacking.

Herzl put his views into a book, little larger than a pamphlet, *Der Judenstaat*. This book found readers in quarters with which he was barely acquainted. His book, the result of his discovery of the Jewish Question, led him to the discovery of the Jewish People. University students are always as a body enthusiastic, eager to accept and forward new ideas, and generally tinged with extremism. Jewish students are no different from others, except that perhaps they are more so. It has been very truly said of the Jews that they are just like other people, only more so, and Jewish students are like other students, only perhaps more so. The dream of Palestine, as has been shown on an earlier page, has always been existent in Jewry. Among the young one would expect it to be more vivid than among the older. Nationalism also inevitably makes a keener appeal to the young, students and others, than to their more sober elders. Among the Jewish student societies of the European universities and also among the *Chovevé Zion* societies, which were by now numerous and well scattered, *Der Judenstaat*, fell on fertile soil. It told its readers much that they had dreamed but had been unable to express themselves. But it differed in one respect from their dreams. Herzl's nationalism was Zionism possibly without Zion. The *Chovevé* Zionists would have accepted Zion without Zionism, but would not forgo Zion in any circumstances. The publication of the book brought these classes, men and Jews of whom Herzl had hitherto but a dim knowledge, into contact with him. They were willing to range themselves behind him, to give him a party and a platform without which he knew that all his efforts must prove futile, provided that he would accept Zion and discard all alternatives. To Herzl the offer seemed well worth accepting and he took it. Henceforth, he gave the remaining nine years of his life wholeheartedly to his new cause, sacrificing his family, his fortune, his health, in the end his life. Apart from those who were possessed by the thoughtlessness of youth, Herzl's new army certainly contained some convinced nationalists who were political Zionists. On the other hand there were also some who were equally convinced anti-nationalists. The great bulk of the new party, like the great mass of mankind, had no real views, since, also in this no exception, they never thought things out. Caught by a shibboleth, a catchword, flattered by the invitation of a cynosure of the West, dazzled by Herzl's strikingly handsome appearance and natural attraction, they trooped to his recruiting stations and almost overnight he found himself the head of a great party in Jewry.

Herzl's Zionism was essentially political and in this differed altogether from that of the *Chovevé Zion* and of the Jewish leaders of Europe and America who had encouraged or put forward Palestine programmes at intervals during the nineteenth century. He wanted a Jewish state, similar to other national states, except that its inhabitants or nationals would be Jews. Jewish settlement in Palestine was not so much a matter of immediate consequence as political security. First must come, in his mind, an international treaty under which the Porte would recognize Palestine as a Jewish state —not necessarily outside of the Ottoman Empire in which it might be in a sense a protectorate—a Jewish National Home. Once this was secured, tied together threefold, development and Jewish settlement would follow. He felt that all development previous to the security of absolute safeguards would only increase the value of the country to the Turk and raise his price. He was not prepared to develop other people's property until he had bought the freehold or had at least secured a very long lease. Cultural Zionism or Spiritual Zionism, the revival or development of a Jewish civilization, one of which he knew nothing except in a material sense, had also little appeal for him. Jewish nationalism, using the term in its current sense, it is interesting to note, is in a sense the supreme instance of assimilation, although its advocates seem quite unconscious of that fact. It is a movement to divest Jewry of its peculiar attributes and to make it 'as other nations', a community of individuals with a common history, a common tradition, a common language, bound together politically, self-conscious and actively or latently hostile to all other peoples. The Mission of Israel whatever it may be, the justification for the survival of the Jewish people during the past two thousand years is to be abandoned in a moment and the number of small weak states, whose existence to-day is fraught with so much misery in the world is to be increased by one. The Jewish Nationalists, the Political Zionists, are in reality among the most assimilated of the Jews. They also have succumbed to their environment. In fact the Nationalists have adopted the Nazi contention that a Jew cannot be a German. Rabbi Israel Mattuck has diagnosed Jewish Nationalism in a few but penetrating words. 'Modern Jewish Nationalism is not an inner product of Jewish life. It is the result of a modern European development and the circumstances of the Jews. It is partly European nationalism applied to the Jews, and partly the result of pressure on the Jews by Anti-Semitism, which itself is in its modern form a product of nationalism. Jewish Nationalism and Anti-Semitism are two branches of the same tree, or, perhaps it would be a more appropriate figure, two currents from the same dynamo, and they affect one another. They are both related to the growth of Nationalism in the modern world. They both look upon the Jews as a distinctive nation.'[1]

One of Herzl's first steps on accepting the leadership of the Movement was to convene a congress in Basle in August 1897 at which the Zionist Organisation was formed. In this Congress Jews from half the countries of the world participated. The aim of the Movement was formulated in the 'Basle Programme', 'Zionism aims at establishing for the Jewish people a home in Palestine secured by public law.' The means by which this object was to be attained were a compromise between the views of Herzl and the other Political Zionists and those of the *Chovevé Zion*, which had been absorbed by the new Movement and to whom the creation of a Jewish state was of secondary if of any consequence. The means as formulated were (*a*) the settlement of Jewish agriculturists, artizans and labourers in Palestine, (*b*) the organization and binding together of the whole of Jewry, subject to the laws of the countries in which they dwelt, (*c*) the strengthening and fostering of Jewish national sentiment and consciousness, and (*d*) the taking of preliminary steps towards obtaining the agreement of governments necessary for the attainment of the aim of Zionism.

[1] I. I. Mattuck, *What are the Jews?* page 68.

POLITICAL ZIONISM

Herzl's first public appeal had been to the Jews of England. He had come to London in July 1896 and put his proposals before the Maccabaeans—half a club, half a society of Jewish professional men interested in Jewish problems—but had had a very critical reception. Anglo-Jewry wanted to have nothing to do with any sort of political Judaism. Herzl was keenly disappointed, for he had hoped to make London the centre of his new movement. A few days later he had a more successful meeting in the East End of London, where his audience was mainly foreign, closely akin in all respects to the masses of the Russian Pale of Settlement where Judaism was more living and the Jewish need more urgent, and also the sense of political reality little developed. It was however clear that no help was forthcoming from Anglo-Jewry and even among the foreign Jewish population of England there was little active Zionist interest until the issue of the Balfour Declaration twenty years later made Zionism not only a matter of Jewish but also of British concern. Outside of England also, in those early days, Herzl obtained little support except from the masses. Almost the only outstanding Jews who came to his banner, those whose names were known outside their own countries, were Max Nordau and the brothers Marmorek in Paris, Moses Gaster and Israel Zangwill in London, and Richard Gottheil in New York. Apart from them Herzl stood alone. And they had other interests and moreover were separated from him and from Vienna by thousands of miles.

In all eleven Zionists Congresses were held before the outbreak of war in 1914 and every one saw an increased and more extensive Jewish representation.

Gradually the Jewish rabbinical or religious prejudice against the Movement weakened. Although no religious test was imposed for the admission of Jews to the Movement and many of its members and especially of its leaders were far removed from traditional Judaism, the Rabbis discovered that they and their followers were not excluded. Herzl was sincerely desirous of making his Movement all-embracing so far as Jews were concerned, and welcomed the Conservatives as well as the Liberals. Even at the beginning a few rabbis had come in. Ultimately a religiously observant party was formed within the organization, the *Mizrachi*, whose special function it is to watch over the interests of Judaism within Zionism. Nevertheless there has always been a party in Jewry that looked upon the Zionist Movement and Organisation almost as godless and blasphemous inasmuch as they proposed to force the hands of Providence. That the Jews will return to Palestine and prosper there they are as convinced as any Zionist, but no human agency can secure this end or even help towards it. It will come in God's good time and then only by divine means. They do not share the view that God helps those who help themselves.

Herzl devoted the seven years between the first Zionist Congress and his premature death mostly to diplomatic activity. His object was to secure a charter for the settlement of Jews in Palestine and for their self-government. As a means to that end he hoped for the raising of a Jewish National fund. The latter project however concerned the Jews. He made several visits to Constantinople and had more than one interview with the Sultan. By the German Emperor he was

POLITICAL ZIONISM

received twice, on one occasion in Palestine. Herzl was also received in audience by the King of Italy and the Pope. In 1903 he was in St. Petersburg to persuade the Russian Government to withdraw its prohibition on Zionist activities. By all these rulers he was received with fair words and other expressions of sympathy, but nowhere had he any practical encouragement. The Powers, whether they considered him an idealist dreamer or realized that although he was more than that there was no power behind him, never took him seriously, a man of great charm and interest with whom conversation was a pleasure, but nothing more. To this rule there was one exception. The British Government, with the Palestine tradition behind it, did give more consideration to Herzl and his Movement. After his abortive visit at the outset of his Zionist activities, he came again to the country in 1900 when a Zionist Congress was held in London in a vain further attempt to attract the Anglo-Jewish leaders, and in 1902 to give evidence and put his views before the Royal Commission that was considering the question of alien immigration, largely a Jewish problem. Whether or not he came into touch with British statesmen on either of these occasions or on a later one when he was the private guest of Lord Rothschild, the head of the Anti-Zionist party in Anglo-Jewry, is not known. Not long afterwards, however, the suggestion came from the British Government of a possible Jewish settlement in the district of El Arish in the Sinai peninsula, Egyptian territory, but geographically part of Palestine. The Zionist Organisation sent out a commission of inquiry to investigate the possibilities. The Commission damned the proposal with very faint praise. El Arish is after all but a small oasis in a desert, with little opportunity for expansion. Yet Jews, above all Zionists, always optimists, ready, generally forced, to clutch at straws, might have pursued the matter further, if the Egyptian Government had not become nervous at the suggestion of a new land of Goshen. Thus the offer lapsed. The El Arish project and its failure led, however, direct to another offer by the British Government which if it had been accepted might have diverted the trend of Jewish history.

The first years of the twentieth century were those of the very beginning of the British East African Empire. The wide region now known as Kenya, although under British control was to a large extent unknown, with a very small white population. Joseph Chamberlain, the very active and alert British Colonial Secretary, on the way to visit the British South African Empire, stopped at Mombasa to see this new patrimony. It attracted him as enshrining much promise. Although El Arish was not within his province, as a member of the Cabinet, he was acquainted with the projected settlement there and of the abandonment of the proposal. East Africa also was under the Foreign Office in those days. But the Jews were in Chamberlain's mind when he viewed this new African land, one apparently of great agricultural wealth and with no white population. The possibility of Jewish settlement there occurred to him and when he returned to England some weeks later, he spoke to the Foreign Secretary, Lord Lansdowne, on the subject, and as a consequence, on 14 August 1903, Lord Landsowne made a formal offer, on behalf of the

POLITICAL ZIONISM

British Government, to the Zionist Organisation, of territory in British East Africa, now Kenya, on which to establish an autonomous Jewish settlement.[1] Lansdowne in his letter making the offer, stated that he had 'studied the question with the interest which His Majesty's Government must always take in any well-considered scheme for the amelioration of the position of the Jewish race.' He then proceeded to give some details of the offer which were open for discussion. 'A considerable area of land' was to be allocated. A Jewish official was to be appointed head of the administration and the settlement was to be given municipal freedom and self-government and similar freedom and self-government in 'religious and purely domestic matters, such local autonomy being conditional upon the right of His Majesty's Government to exercise general control'.

This offer put Herzl in a very difficult position. He had never been wedded to Palestine as the only land for his prospective state and his long record of failure must inevitably have aroused in him a feeling of pessimism, that Palestine was unattainable by the Jewish people. The new offer was in itself a very generous one and very tempting. On the face of it it gave everything that he had originally put forward as his aim, with the additional, overwhelming advantage of a state being founded and growing up under British protection. Not much was known of East Africa and some investigations would have to be made before a decision could be reached, but at any rate to the uninformed observer the site

[1] This is generally referred to as the Uganda project, but the offer related to no part of the Uganda protectorate.

of the proposed settlement seemed to offer many advantages and great promise. On the other hand East Africa was not Palestine. It had neither Jewish history, nor Jewish sentiment, nor the Jewish religion behind it. To most of the Jews of the world, one might say, the region was not known to exist. To them it had no past, no present and as far as they knew no future. The Zionist Movement had its very centre in Palestine. Remove the centre, take Zion away and could there, would there, be any Movement remaining? It was true that Herzl's followers were a somewhat heterogeneous collection, many of the prominent ones being like him, Jewish nationalists rather than Zionists, but the Zionists, those to whom Palestine meant everything and no other possible country anything, were numerous, very numerous, perhaps numerous enough to wreck the Movement and the Organisation if an attempt were made to turn it away from Jerusalem. Apart from all these considerations the British offer was one unique in Jewish history. Apart from anything else, it meant the recognition of the Zionist Organisation by a Great Power and by that Great Power to which Jewry had always looked as its friend, without whose sympathy Herzl had always felt no measure of success anywhere was possible. An offer of such a character, from such a source, could not be rejected out of hand. There were many reasons why Herzl would have liked to accept the offer, but dare he do so? On the other hand could he refuse it without doing irreparable harm to his cause, and perhaps also to the interests of Jewry?

The offer was made in August, 1903, on the eve of a Zionist Congress, and was of course submitted to it.

POLITICAL ZIONISM

Herzl's recommendation was a compromise or at least a postponement of a decision. The course that he advocated was an expression of gratitude to the British Government for the offer and for the practical sympathy and thoughtfulness that were behind it. Such an offer however could not be accepted without deep consideration and it was desired therefore to defer a decision while the possibilities of the proposed region of settlement were being investigated. The compromise that was in Herzl's mind was that although East Africa was not Zion it might be accepted as a half-way house. a *Nachtasyl* as he termed it, in which the Jewish wanderers of Europe could find refuge and rest while on the journey to the Holy Land. Just as their ancestors needed the training of forty years in the Wilderness before they were fitted to take up their inheritance, so the Jews of to-day should also have a period of training in East Africa to fit them for their restoration in Palestine. To put the position bluntly, Herzl, exhausted by his efforts and disappointments, with no real objection to East Africa, longed for 'Peace in our time.' He thought the British offer would give it. But he was mistaken.

The East European Jew is as a rule emotional. Of the members of a Zionist Congress the great majority are always East European. To the East European Zionist also, with few exceptions, the alternatives are Palestine or nothing. In many cases, imbued with the Russian point of view, compromise was inconceivable. It must be Palestine or nothing. Any other course, they considered in their extravagance, almost treason to the Jewish cause. Opinion in the Congress was decidedly anti-East African. But there was Herzl on the other side, a great influence of himself and of what he had done in creating the Zionist Movement and in raising it from the slums of the Ghetto as high as Whitehall and the Wilhelmstrasse. Herzl had already performed miracles. He was capable of still others. Even the most violent advocate of Zion or nothing realized that without Herzl it would be nothing, whereas with him it might be Zion. The struggle was roughly between East and West in Zionism. The West wanted to accept the offer if only as a temporary measure: the East was resolutely opposed to touching even the heretical proposal. In the end Herzl's great influence was successful in persuading a number of the Eastern Zionists to agree to the sending of a commission of investigation to East Africa. These were sufficient to give him a majority. but the minority, irreconcilable and hysterical, went into mourning, feeling and believing that all was lost, that the vision of Zion had faded away, from their eyes at any rate, for ever. To show their hesitations and doubts even the majority could not be got to agree to the cost of the commission of investigation coming from Zionist funds. The money required had to be obtained elsewhere. The Commission was to report to a Zionist Congress in the following year and this was to make a final decision. Before that Congress Herzl had died, at the age of forty-four, worn out by his efforts on behalf of the Jewish people.

The Congress met at Basle in July 1905, but it was a congress without a leader, without a dominating personality accepted as Herzl had been by all. His obvious successor was Max Nordau, a man with an even greater international reputation than Herzl's, orator and leader of opinion with followings in all the countries of the civilized world, but Nordau did not want the office. Perhaps he realized that a supporter of the East African scheme, which he was, could not be at the head of the Zionist Movement: perhaps he felt that, although an outstanding orator and writer he was yet no statesman, hardly a diplomatist: the reasons for his refusal may have been purely personal and private. Failing Nordau, Moses Gaster was a great man in Jewry and in Zionism and one moreover untouched by the East African heresy. But Gaster had his difficulties with his own community in London, the *Sephardim*, of whom he was the Chief Rabbi, who were opposed to a man to the whole of Zionism, its politics and its ways. Moreover there was a feeling among Zionists, members of a secular movement, that a cleric should not be their chief. Zionists have always as a body been very shy of clericalism. A third possibility, a smaller man yet one with an international reputation and above all an Englishman, a great qualification then among the Zionists, was Israel Zangwill, but he also was tainted with the East African heresy, and moreover faults of temperament made him obviously unfitted to lead a movement such as that of the Zionists. There was no other Zionist sufficiently known outside his own country or outstanding even there. Herzl had left no successor. Still someone had to sit in his chair. For this purpose one of his supporters from the beginning, a Russian Jew who had settled in Germany and made a moderate fortune there in commerce, David Wolffsohn, was chosen, but everyone knew that Wolffsohn had not picked up the mantle of Herzl, and if he had, it was too large for him.

Even before Herzl's death the Russian Zionists, those opposed not only to East Africa but restive for other reasons, doubtful about the virtues of political Zionism and considering that colonization of Jews in Palestine was of more value than interviews and promises from all the statesmen of Europe, had been holding conferences. The nucleus of these were the old *Chovevé* Zionists, the Zionists before Herzl, who had suspended their activities somewhat halfheartedly, but had never abandoned them. They organized themselves for the forthcoming congress, that at which the decision, as they put it, between Zion and Uganda, had to be taken. When they came to it they found themselves the one strong party, with only a congeries of individuals outside of their circle. The report of the investigating commission was placed before this Congress. The Commission seemed to be in doubt whether or not the offered territory could support a large population. But the report had in effect no consideration. The question was a political, not an economic one. The influence and awe of Herzl were also missing. The majority was overwhelmingly on the side of the Zionist purists. So small was the minority that its members refrained from voting. The Congress therefore resolved without opposition, first that the fundamental principle of the Movement was the colonization of Palestine and the adjacent lands and nowhere else. While declining the British offer it thanked the Government for having made it and expressed the hope that Britain would continue to give its good office to the Movement in furtherance of its programme as laid down at Basle and just confirmed. This Congress was epoch-making in another respect. The minority, although it did not vote, was deeply disappointed. It still held that the rescue of the Jewish people was worth far more than the gratifying of Jewish sentiment in Palestine. It considered the East African offer as one of outstanding promise, which it was a crime against the Jewish people to have rejected. Their fellow-Zionists they considered a collection of impractical visionaries who would always sacrifice the substance for the shadow. They therefore withdrew from all further co-operation with them and under the leadership of Zangwill formed a rival organization, the Jewish Territorial Organization, whose object was to find a territory anywhere on which a Jewish self-governing community could be built. Zangwill found a certain amount of support in England, America and elsewhere outside the Zionist Movement, especially among men who had the confidence of their fellow-Jews. Several proposals in Cyrenaica, Angola and elsewhere were investigated—East Africa was no longer available for mass Jewish settlement—but rejected as unsuitable. The one concrete work of the new organization, known briefly as the Ito, was the direction of Jewish emigration to the United States of America away from New York and other congested Jewish centres, and its dispersion. Otherwise it performed no task. Gradually its activities lessened until after the War and the opening of the new era in Zionism the Ito faded away. It may be said to have done nothing practical except to guide one man, David Eder, from the extreme of assimilation to a seat of leadership in Zionism in its new post-War phase.

After Herzl the history of Zionism passed into an

era of small men until the upheaval of the Great War brought a new generation to the top. Inside the Movement there were struggles between the Political and the 'Practical' Zionists in which the latter succeeded in gaining control. But with small men and few opportunities little could be done. Political activity fell into the background. A few small Jewish agricultural settlements were founded and supported with great difficulty. In Palestine also, in the last days of the Peace era, there was a widespread revolt in Jewry against attempts at German Jewish domination of the growing community. The Jews of Eastern Europe were always jealous of their fellow-Jews of Germany and the dislike was generally reciprocated.

CHAPTER VI

THE BALFOUR DECLARATION

The War of 1914: Chaim Weizmann: Influential British Interest: The Sykes-Picot Treaty: The Arab Question: The Balfour Declaration: Its Meaning: The Motives: Mr. Lloyd George's Views: Zionism and Bolshevism: The Anti-Zionists: The Arab Attitude: The Hogarth Message: The Supposed Price of the Balfour Declaration: The British Non-Zionists.

THE OUTBREAK of war in 1914 created a crisis for the Zionist Movement as for all international organizations. Its headquarters in Berlin were at once cut off from all its branches and members in the Allied and, for practical purposes also, in neutral countries. Its activities came in effect to a standstill. One of the members of the Executive happened to be in America and a Provisional Executive of the Zionist Organisation was formed by him in New York. This was useful later in supporting a self-appointed group that took charge of affairs in London and in getting influential American sympathy for its aims and objects. Above all, the American Zionists raised the funds by which the starving Jews of Palestine were supported, and kept in existence as much as possible of the Jewish creations in the Holy Land. In England there was none of the Zionist leaders. Gaster was in political retirement, Zangwill in opposition. There was a sprinkling of members of the Greater Actions Committee, the large body that met normally in inter-Congress years and conducted the humdrum affairs of the Organisation. But with one exception these were of no consequence in the larger Jewish world, past, present or future. The one exception was Dr. Chaim Weizmann, a Manchester lecturer in bio-chemistry, Polish-born, who had settled in England some years earlier. As a student in Berlin and Freiburg and later as a teacher in Switzerland, he had thrown himself into the Zionist Movement, ranging himself with his fellow Russian Zionists, the purists, to whom Zion can be only in Palestine. His master had been and was Ahad Ha'Am who had been living in London for some years, but who had taken no active part in the Zionist Organisation or the Movement since the First Congress. Weizmann was an Ahad Ha'Am Zionist or a 'Spiritual' Zionist. He was also a 'Practical' Zionist, one to whom the settlement of Jews in Palestine and their free self-supporting life there were of more consequence than political concessions. For him it was sufficient, at any rate for the present, if the Jews devoted themselves to education and colonization. The establishment of a Hebrew University in Jerusalem was the great work to which Ahad Ha'Am and Weizmann looked forward, for to its care they would entrust the soul of the Jewish people.

When war broke out between Britain and Turkey in November 1914, Dr. Weizmann was still in Manchester. The outbreak of war and the declaration by the Prime Minister immediately afterwards that it meant 'the death-knell of Ottoman dominion, not only in Europe, but in Asia' made for Englishmen, Gentiles and Jews, Zionism in a moment a practical question.

If the Ottoman Empire in Asia was to be liquidated, Palestine would change masters. With the change the opportunity of the Zionists would come. Who knew but that the treaty of peace would mark the reappearance after the lapse of many centuries of a Jewish homeland in Palestine? As to what Zionism meant or wanted most people in England, Jews as well as others, were very hazy at that time. Everybody gave his own definition to it and almost everybody was sympathetic, to his own form of Zionism. Thus all England was Zionist, in one sense of another.

The outbreak of war with Turkey announced the hour and in Dr. Weizmann providence provided the man to seize it. Among his friends in Manchester was Charles Prestwich Scott, the Editor of the *Manchester Guardian*, who had either through Dr. Weizmann or otherwise, become interested in Zionism. With a Liberal Government in power Scott, as the Editor of the most influential Liberal newspaper, was a man who counted. Armed with an introduction from him Dr. Weizmann came to London and sought an interview with Mr. Lloyd George, then Chancellor of the Exchequer and the second man in the Government. The interview was readily granted. At it, at Mr. Lloyd George's suggestion, was Mr. (now Viscount) Samuel, the Home Secretary who happened to be a Jew. Mr. Samuel had hitherto taken no part in Jewish public affairs, nor had Zionism apparently appealed in any way to him. He was a practical politician, not a dreamer. But he also realized that the war with Turkey had effected a great change, that Zionism was possibly on the point of stepping out of the academic sphere into that of practical politics. As a practical policy it was worth considering. A result of the interview at any rate was the awakening by Dr. Weizmann of the interest of the two statesmen. An interview not long afterwards with Balfour, then the most influential British statesman outside the Government, seemed to revive the interest he had shown eight years earlier when Weizmann had had a talk with him on the subject.

Weizmann's task seemed clear, to convert British public men to a sympathetic attitude towards Zionist ideals so that when the opportunity came their sympathy could be translated into practical steps. In this he was remarkably successful. Nahum Sokolow, a Russian member of the Zionist Executive, soon came to England to co-operate with Weizmann in this work. A small group of young English Zionists, reinforced by a few older ones including Ahad Ha'Am, gathered round them as advisers and assistants. Weizmann also came to London as Director of the Admiralty Laboratories. Balfour shortly afterwards became First Lord of the Admiralty and thus a means of frequent contact outside of the political sphere was created. However in another direction also another and more effective means of contact between the Government and the Zionists was created. Sir Mark Sykes, a young Conservative member of Parliament with a considerable knowledge of the Middle East and its affairs, was charged by the Foreign Office with keeping an eye on that part of the world and its problems. He was especially interested in the relations with the Arabs and the Armenians and their future. A study of Arab problems at once brought him to Palestine and at Palestine Zionism and the Jews of course appeared. The obvious next step was to make contact with Zionists in England. He approached the Editor

THE BALFOUR DECLARATION

of the *Jewish Chronicle*, Leopold Greenberg, who was one of the old Zionists but had as a Herzlian Zionist been for some years in political retirement. By him Sykes was introduced to Gaster who also had not been active in Zionism for some years. Zionism in England was as a matter of fact moribund at this time. It was in Gaster's house in February 1917 that Sykes met for the first time Weizmann and Sokolow and a small group of other sympathizers, some avowed Zionists, some not. From this meeting onwards the conversations that ended in the official sponsoring of Zionism by the British Government were conducted by Sykes on the one side and Weizmann and Sokolow on the other. Jechiel Tschlenow, another Russian member of the Zionist Executive, who had also come to London, died not long after his arrival.

The talks on the subject were long drawn out. They commenced in February 1917 and ended late in the following October, shortly before the Government pronouncement that came to be known as the Balfour Declaration was issued. Previous to this period, so far from thinking of the creation of a Jewish Palestine according to any interpretation, the British Government did not even contemplate a Palestinian state. The Sykes-Picot Agreement with the French which was negotiated after Weizmann's talks with members of the Cabinet and was signed in the spring of 1916, decided on the carving-up of Palestine into half a dozen fragments. Transjordan was to be part of an Arab state whose centre was to be in Syria. Northern Palestine was to be included in the French protectorate of the Lebanon. The Acre-Haifa district was to become a part of the British Empire. The remainder of the country, a limbless torso, was to be placed under an international administration, Britain, France and Russia apparently to be the joint guardians. This remnant contained the Christian Holy Places and incidentally the Moslem ones and most of the Jewish ones also. Neither of the Allies, France, the traditional Protector of the Latins, and Russia, that of the Orthodox, would agree to the other being in control. As a balance Britain was apparently brought in, but Britain had an interest of her own in the proximity of the Suez Canal. Neither France nor Russia nor Britain seems ever at this time to have thought of the Jews in connexion with Palestine.

The ink on the Sykes-Picot Treaty was hardly dry when one of its authors began to look round for means of cancelling it. He had in the meanwhile discovered the Jews and an international truncated Palestine could in no way fit in with the realization of the Zionist ideal as conceived by any party in Jewry. A Jewish community in any Zionist sense was inconceivable with Russia, the arch-persecutor of the Jews, in even part control of it. Moreover Jewish sentiment in all countries had always and for very good reasons been sympathetic towards Britain, and Jews everywhere felt that if a new Jewish era in Palestine were to be given a fair chance of developing, it could be only under British protection. In Zionism there were many parties, each with its own idea of the ideal constitution for Palestine. None doubted for a moment—even the most extreme and unrealistic of the nationalists—that Palestine Jewry would need a protector and every one of them felt that Britain was the only protector they could trust. By this time Sykes had become a strong

THE BALFOUR DECLARATION

Zionist sympathizer and he shared the views that if there were to be any Jewish future in Palestine it could be only under British protection. Thus there were two series of talks that had to be concluded before a Palestine settlement could be envisaged. France and Russia would have to be persuaded to cancel the Sykes-Picot Treaty: A formula acceptable to the Zionists and one the British could also accept would have to be found. There was a third party, the Arabs, with which conversations were also being conducted, with Palestine, however, only an incident. An agreement with them was ultimately reached, one which left Palestine an open question, or, according to another interpretation, believed, by a most unfortunate misunderstanding, to be settled. However, an Arab revolt against Turkey was a matter of urgency, far more urgent than the resolution of either of the other two questions. The general principle of an Arab revolt and a British-Arab alliance was agreed to, the details, including the future of Palestine, being left over for settlement when there was more leisure. The negotiations with France and Russia were eased by the Bolshevik Revolution and the disappearance of Russia from the Middle Eastern scene. Negotiations with France were somewhat protracted, but in the end, somewhat grudgingly, her Government agreed to disinterest herself in Palestine and to withdraw not quite to the natural limits of the Lebanon but almost as far. All south of her new protectorates she acknowledged as a British sphere of interest. Thus there was a practically intact Palestine in which it was possible to build up a Jewish National Home, a centre for Jewry, even a Jewish state.

There remained the talks with the Zionists and the

formulation of the Balfour Declaration. This document in its final form runs 'His Majesty's Government view with favour the establishment in Palestine of a national home for the Jewish people, and will use their best endeavours to facilitate the achievement of this object, it being clearly understood that nothing shall be done which may prejudice the civil and religious rights of non-Jewish communities in Palestine, or the rights and political status enjoyed by Jews in any other country.'

At once the indefiniteness and vagueness of the wording of the Declaration leaps to the eye. It was obviously the result of a compromise and compromises may be workable but compromise documents are almost always unsatisfactory. In the first place the term 'A national home for the Jewish people' is indefinite. It has no exact meaning. There was no precedent for its use. Here again every one was justified in reading almost any meaning he wished into it. And far more than was intended was read into it at once, especially by those who jump to conclusions without troubling to consider the premises. This was especially the case among the Zionists of America who could conceive of no 'national home' that was not a political state and also among the Jews of Eastern Europe. The issue of the Declaration let loose a flood of political nationalism, especially among those Jews who, in consequence of the political systems under which they lived and their special disabilities as Jews, had been politically starved, a starvation aggravated by their knowledge, in most cases superficial, but none the less vivid on that account, of the political systems of the Western States. With the issue of the Balfour Declaration a frenzy seemed to carry a great part of Jewry off its feet. Palestine had not yet even been conquered, yet a Salonica Jewish periodical, within a few weeks of the issue of the Declaration, announced the formation of a Jewish cabinet for the government of Palestine, and gave the names of its members—Sokolow, Zangwill and other prominent Jews who were known to be more or less sympathetic with Zionism in one or other of its interpretations. Even official Zionist bodies got so involved in the excitement as to make absurdly extravagant statements supported by alleged official backing. One such was in a pamphlet issued by the New York Provisional Committee for Zionist Affairs, a body of considerable authority in Zionism. In a pamphlet which it issued early in 1917 it published an 'extract from a proclamation issued by General Sir Archibald Murray', then Commander-in-Chief of the Egypt Expeditionary Force. 'There can be little doubt that we should revive the Jewish Palestine of old, and allow the Jews to realise their dreams of Zion in their own homeland. All the Jews will not return to Palestine, but many will do so. The new Jewish state, under British or French ægis, would become the spiritual and cultural centre of Jewry throughout the world. The Jews would at least have a homeland and a nationality of their own.'[1] The more responsible and sober-minded Zionists in England who could learn nothing of this extraordinary 'proclamation' at once inquired the authority for the quotation, but it seems could get no information. It was so obviously apocryphal that there was no need to contradict it. But in America it did not pass into the oblivion it deserved. Jacob de Haas, a very prominent

[1] *Palestine*, Vol. II., page 16, 4 August, 1917.

American Zionist who claimed to have been the mentor of Herzl and also of ex-Justice Brandeis, elaborated this fairy tale. In his biography of Justice Brandeis[1] he mentions a 'British Official War Book' from which he quotes as the British official terms for the settlement of Palestine, 'Palestine to be recognized as the Jewish National Home. Jews of all countries to be accorded full liberty of immigration. Jews to enjoy full national, political and civic rights according to their place of residence in Palestine. A Charter to be granted to a Jewish Company for the development of Palestine. The Hebrew language to be recognized as the official language of the Jewish province.' Much of this is obscure, but the general tendency is clear. In a footnote de Haas gave 'a detailed statement by the British War Department in April 1917' which is apparently an elaboration of the foregoing.

'It is proposed that the following be adopted as the heads of a scheme for a Jewish re-settlement of Palestine in accordance with Jewish National Aspirations:

'1. BASIS OF SETTLEMENT. Recognition of Palestine as the Jewish National Home.

'2. STATUS OF JEWISH POPULATION IN PALESTINE GENERALLY. The Jewish population present and future throughout Palestine is to possess and enjoy full national, political and civic rights.

'3. IMMIGRATION INTO PALESTINE. The Suzerain Government shall grant full and free rights of immigration into Palestine to Jews of all countries.

[1] *Louis Dembitz Brandeis*, pp. 89-90.

THE BALFOUR DECLARATION

'4. THE ESTABLISHMENT OF A CHARTERED COMPANY. The Suzerain Government shall grant a charter to a Jewish Company for the colonization and development of Palestine, the Company to have power to acquire and take over any concessions for works of a public character, which may have been or may hereafter be granted by the Suzerain Government and the rights of pre-emption of Crown Lands or other lands not held in private or religious ownership and such other powers and privileges as are usual in Charters or Statutes of similar colonizing bodies.

'5. COMMUNAL AUTONOMY. Full autonomy is to be enjoyed by Jewish Communities throughout Palestine in all matters bearing upon their educational, religious or communal welfare.'

The document bears a close resemblance to one of the earlier Zionist drafts of the Mandate which were rejected by the British Government. It will be noticed that the full flight of the author's imagination did not as yet quite reach the goal of a Jewish state.

In the following year, 1930, appeared another book with the not very polite title *The Great Betrayal* for which de Haas in collaboration with Rabbi Stephen Wise, a still more important American Zionist, was also responsible. In this book the alleged 'British War Department statement on the War Aims in the Near East', was repeated, and we are then told that the five preliminary sentences which were a crystallization of the longer official statement were the work of 'Allied War propagandists' so that 'all who run might read what

England proposed'. They look more like the extravagant propaganda of irresponsible Zionists into whose heads the intoxication of the expected Balfour Declaration had risen. The Jews of England were spared a similar folly. They knew that whatever a National Home meant it did not mean a Jewish state, at any rate during the lives of men and women then living. Gaster, described by Lawrence as 'one of the extreme Zionists,' was reported by Professor William Yale, one of the United States delegation to Paris for the peace-making, to have said that 'Zionism was a dead letter: that the Arab movement had reached such large dimensions it was impossible to create a Jewish state . . . that "the British and Zionists had made a bargain and the Zionists had gotten the worst of it"'.[1]

There were many in England who knew of the arguments and controversies around the alternatives 'a' and 'the' as a prefix to 'National Home'. The situation has been succinctly summarized by Ahad Ha'Am who will be quoted later. There was also the reference to 'the civil and religious rights of non-Jewish communities in Palestine' and the pious expression ordaining the safeguarding of 'the rights and political status enjoyed by Jews in any other country', inserted in recognition of the fears of those who felt that any shadow of a suggestion of a political status for Jews as Jews must react unfavourably on the position of the Jews everywhere or almost everywhere. The Zionists would of course have preferred a 'declaration' much stronger and more definite. The Non-Zionists or Anti-Zionists were nervous of the whole thing, thinking more of the great Jewry of the Dispersion than of the small Jewish popula-

[1] *The Letters of T. E. Lawrence*, p. 285.

THE BALFOUR DECLARATION

tion that could in the most favourable circumstances find a home in Palestine. The British Government, in a sense, sympathized with both parties and tried to satisfy them, but even Balfour himself, writing a year after the issue of his Declaration, was very careful not to raise any hopes of anything of the nature of a Jewish political state. It is true he did not rule out any such development. The most that can be said is that he left the question open.[1] According to Mr. Lloyd George he held these views when the Declaration was approved by the Cabinet. 'As to the meaning of the words "national home" ... he (Balfour) understood it to mean some form of British, American or other protectorate, under which full facilities would be given to the Jews to work out their own salvation and to build up, by means of education, agriculture and industry, a real centre of national culture and focus of national life. It did not necessarily involve the early establishment of an independent Jewish state, which was a matter for gradual development in accordance with the ordinary laws of political evolution.'[2]

Five years later, in a debate in the House of Lords in reply to a suggestion that a 'Jewish National Home', as interpreted in the Mandate and by the British Government, meant a Jewish domination over the Arabs, speaking with some heat, Balfour resented the suggestion that the British Government or its representative or the Mandates Commission of the League would tolerate the oppression and domination of one section of the population by another. 'I cannot imagine any political interests exercised under greater safeguards

[1] See pp. XXIX et seq. of Vol I of N. Sokolow's *History of Zionism*.
[2] David Lloyd George, *The Truth about the Peace Treaties*, p. 1137.

than the political interests of the Arab population of Palestine.' Later in the same speech, after appealing for a chance for the Jews to show whether they can in Palestine, without injury to others, 'organize a culture in a Home where it will be secured from oppression', he continued, that if they succeeded 'we should then have given them what every other nation has, some place, some local habitation, where they can develop the culture and the traditions which are peculiarly their own.'[1]

This programme of Balfour's differed little if at all from the official one put before the Cabinet by the Zionist spokesmen, speaking through the mouth of the second Lord Rothschild who was at that time entirely under Zionist influence. According to Mr. Lloyd George it was quoted by Lord Curzon in a cabinet memorandum as 'a home where the Jews could speak their own language, have their own education, their own civilization, and religious institutions under the protection of Allied Governments'. It is only fair to say, however, that there were other Jewish definitions of 'a National Home'. Sir Alfred Mond, afterwards Lord Melchett, quoted at the same time by Curzon, wanted an autonomous Jewish state 'i.e. a political unity, composed of Jews, governed by Jews, and administered mainly in the interests of Jews'. But Mond was a very recent convert not only to Zionism but even to Hebraism. Religiously he never was a Jew. And converts are proverbially far more extreme than men who have been born and brought up in their faith. Moreover Mond never held any office in the Zionist Organisation. Cromer, who was very sympathetic but whose experience

[1] *Speeches on Zionism by the Earl of Balfour*, pp. 47 and 63.

THE BALFOUR DECLARATION

told him where the practicable ended and the impracticable commenced, also preferred a 'Spiritual centre of the Jews' to the more extravagant demands.[1] One of the most reasonable of the English Zionists, writing eight years later, admitted that anything of the nature of a Jewish state, for which a Jewish majority is essential, is inconceivable in our time. 'The Arabs start with so large a numerical majority that even if Jewish immigration plus natural increase continues somewhat to exceed the natural increase of the Arabs, there is still little prospect of the Arabs being overtaken in a numerical sense within a reasonable period of time.'[2]

So far as the British were concerned there was more than one motive behind the Balfour Declaration and one of these was certainly the desire to secure the friendship of the Jews of other countries, neutral and enemy. Of the former the United States of America was not only the most powerful but also the one with the largest Jewish population. The other great Jewish centre was Russia, which although an ally had by then become a somewhat uncertain one. The United States and Russia between them contained half of the Jewish population of the world, not the most politically intelligent and practical half. The American Zionists, in reality few in number and except for a few individuals of eminence, without influence, were for the most part political Zionists. The wealthy and influential Jews of the United States were almost to a man anti-Zionist. To the American Zionists Spiritual Zionism, Ahad

[1] *The Truth about the Peace Treaties*, pp. 1123 to 1132.

[2] L. Stein, *Survey of International Affairs*, 1925, Vol. I., Note 2 (1), p. 392.

98 PALESTINE: A POLICY

Ha'Amism, had no appeal. Few understood its meaning.

As for Russia, if Mr. Lloyd George can be accepted as expressing the opinions held in Government circles at the time, there was a most extraordinary delusion regarding Jewish influence. Not only was the Balfour Declaration to stop the rot that had set in and re-kindle the anti-German ferocity of the Russian people, but it is actually suggested that although the Jews failed to prevent the signature of a treaty of peace, they were a material assistance in depriving the Germans of the benefits of the treaty. In making these extraordinary suggestions no consideration is given to the fact that the overwhelming majority of the Jews of Russia were Ghetto denizens living on the edge of starvation and at the time of which he writes helpless fugitives, scattered over the country, fleeing from the swords and torches and worse of the armies of the Czar and their successors. So far as Jewish Bolsheviks were concerned they were to a man bitterly anti-Zionist as they were opposed to all nationalisms. The anti-Bolshevik Russians—apart from the Jews—were anti-Jewish almost to a man. The Bolsheviks were equally, if not more so, anti-Zionist and anti-Allies, since the Allies were considered the enemies of Bolshevism. The few rich Russian Jews who might once have had some influence were all in hiding, in prison or in exile, so far as they were still alive, and very few of them had Zionist sympathies. In fact, in Russia as elsewhere in those days, the Zionists formed only a minority of the Jews, although it must be admitted that there as elsewhere the Balfour Declaration was the greatest recruiting agent for Zionism ever known.

THE BALFOUR DECLARATION 99

Referring back to the alleged influence of Zionism over Bolsheviks or prospective Bolsheviks one cannot overlook the extraordinary statement attributed by Mr. Lloyd George to General Sir George MacDonogh at the same meeting of a War Cabinet Committee. 'I see a good many of the Zionists, and one suggested to me the day before yesterday that if the Jewish people did not get what they were asking for in Palestine, we should have the whole of Jewry turning Bolsheviks and supporting Bolshevism in all the other countries as they have done in Russia.' The only possible comment on such nonsense was that of Lord Cecil: 'Yes. I can conceive the Rothschilds leading a Bolshevist mob.'

Some formula had to be invented that would to some extent satisfy the Zionists without committing the British Government to an impossible and undesirable line of action and without definitely alienating the influential anti-Zionists. The term 'National Home' was invented. But the British Government did not undertake to create a National Home, whatever that term might mean. It undertook 'to facilitate the achievement of this object', subject to certain safeguards. The task rested with others, the Jewish people or the Zionists. The British Government promised only its sympathetic encouragement.

The terms of the Balfour Declaration undoubtedly fell short of the wishes even of Dr. Weizmann and his circle. He has a tendency always to take on the complexion of his environment, and this environment had in the meanwhile become more nationalist and less 'spiritual'. The Government in giving them less than what they asked was influenced by those English

100   PALESTINE: A POLICY

Jews in whose hands the direction of Anglo-Jewry rested, the successors and heirs, in some cases the descendants, of Sir Moses Montefiore, Sir Isaac Lyon Goldsmid, Sir David Salomons, Baron Lionel de Rothschild and others by whom Anglo-Jewry had been raised to the enviable, as compared with other Jewries, position it occupied. These English Jews were first and above all loyal British subjects. They were termed in derision and perhaps not without justification, a hundred and twenty per cent British. Above all and at all times they considered themselves British first and foremost and to them the welfare and comfort of the Jews elsewhere was intimately bound up with the absence of any suspicion that they could be politically anything but French, German, American, Russian citizens. Any suggestion of a dual allegiance or another citizenship, above all of a Jewish political citizenship, was anathema to them. They did not realize even the difference between nationality and citizenship, how there were Scottish and Welsh nationals whose nationality did not detract one iota from their British citizenship, nor did they seem to realize that the peoples of Eastern Europe and Western Asia were built up of nationalities, that Russia, Austro-Hungary, the Ottoman Empire were empires of many nationalities if of only one citizenship. In their hundred and twenty per cent loyalty anything that savoured of a Jewish citizenship or even a Jewish nationality was anathema. They wanted a Palestine consisting of Palestinians, some of whom would be Jews, some Moslems, some Christians, but only as a matter of religion. Outside of the synagogue the word Jew had no meaning for them. Their attitude with regard to Palestine was summed up

THE BALFOUR DECLARATION

in a manifesto issued in May 1917 in which after reiterating their deep interest in common with all Jews in the Holy Land and in the welfare of the Jews of the Holy Land, they proceeded to lay down their programme for the future of Palestine. 'This policy aimed primarily at making Palestine a Jewish spiritual centre by securing for the local Jews, and the colonists who might join them, such conditions of life as would best enable them to develop the Jewish genius on lines of its own. Larger political questions, not directly affecting the main purpose, were left to be solved as need and opportunity might render possible.' The Zionist Organisation had been invited to co-operate on these lines but had not responded. The writers of the manifesto then proceeded to put before the Government the policy that they advocated in which they asked for 'the formal recognition of the high historic interest Palestine possesses for the Jewish community, and a public declaration that at the close of the War the Jewish population will be secured in the enjoyment of civil and religious liberty, equal political rights with the rest of the population, reasonable facilities for immigration and colonization, and such municipal privileges in the towns and colonies inhabited by them as may be shown to be necessary.' The Government, in drafting the Declaration in its final form, were not altogether unmindful of the point of view of these English Jews. Their Zionism, and they were also in a sense Zionists, was a philanthropic Zionism. They looked on Palestine as a possible land of refuge for the Jews of Russia, including Poland, and to a less extent Roumania, the only lands, apart from some backward oriental countries, in which Jews then really suffered. In other countries, until very recent years, the disabilities of the Jews were in reality light, although galling to their pride.

Generally speaking the Balfour Declaration aroused great enthusiasm, almost messianic enthusiasm, in some cases, among the Jews everywhere. Among the Arabs, so far as they heard of it, the feeling at the lowest was one of misgiving. The Sherif of Mecca, who had by now been completely involved in the Arab Revolt, asked in effect for explanations and these were forthcoming by the sending of Dr., then Commander, D. G. Hogarth to him at Jedda with a message to the effect that 'Since the Jewish opinion of the world is in favour of a return of Jews to Palestine, and inasmuch as this opinion must remain a constant factor, and, further, as His Majesty's Government view with favour the realisation of this aspiration, His Majesty's Government are determined that in so far as is compatible with the freedom of the existing population, both economic and political, no obstacle should be put in the way of the realisation of this ideal.'[1] This message was delivered at the beginning of 1918, two months after the issue of the Balfour Declaration, of which it was and was intended to be an elucidation. The Declaration and the Message were both issued by the same Government of which Mr. Lloyd George was Prime Minister and Balfour Foreign Secretary. The Message was therefore not an interpretation by a government that had no responsibility for the Declaration. The two must be read together and the latter provided a promise to the Arabs that was missing from the former. It fully reassured the Sherif and his people and the risk of their withdrawal from or lack of enthusiasm for the war was removed.

[1] Cmd. 5964 (1939).

THE BALFOUR DECLARATION

Unfortunately the Message was never published by Britain or in any European language and was therefore unknown out of Arabia. When it was published twenty years later in part and in a paraphrase by Mr. George Antonius, in support of the Arab case, it came as a bombshell to Zionists and non-Zionists.[1] Even the Foreign Office seems to have forgotten all about it. An instance of secret diplomacy, that served its immediate purpose without doing any damage at the time, but with a nemesis following later! This Hogarth message was to a large extent a confirmation of an official communication of the British Government to the Sherif Hussein almost two years earlier. It was made in the following terms in January 1916. 'That so far as Palestine is concerned, we are determined that no people shall be subjected to another, but in view of the fact that . . .' (Two clauses then suggested a special regime for the Holy Places of the three faiths.) 'That since the Jewish opinion of the world is in favour of a return of Jews to Palestine, and inasmuch as this opinion must remain a constant factor, and further, as His Majesty's Government view with favour the realization of this aspiration, His Majesty's Government are determined that in so far as is compatible with the freedom of the existing population, both economic and political, no obstacle should be put in the way of the realization of this ideal.'[2]

That this policy, as interpreted in successive pronouncements, was satisfactory to the Arabs there is no room to doubt nor had they any objections to Jewish immigration, within the limits of that policy. Of this there is

[1] It was then published in full by the British Government.
[2] *The Truth about the Peace Treaties*, pp. 1141-2.

much evidence. Mr. George Antonius, who is entitled to speak with authority, says[1] that Husain, in reply to the Message conveyed by Hogarth, said that 'in so far as the aim of the Balfour Declaration was to provide a refuge to Jews from persecution, he would use all his influence to further that aim.' As a practical step he caused an article to be published in *al-Qibla*[2] of Mecca, his official organ, exhorting his people 'to welcome the Jews as brethren and co-operate with them for the common welfare.' T. E. Lawrence, in a report written for the information of the Cabinet in November 1918, said that the Arabs in Palestine would not approve Jewish independence but would 'support as far as they can Jewish infiltration, if it is behind a British, as opposed to an international façade'.[3] This report and this very passage were quoted by Curzon at a meeting of the War Cabinet Eastern Committee the following month[4] when the decision regarding Palestine was under consideration. These opinions must have influenced the Cabinet, for it was at the same meeting that Lord (then Lord Robert) Cecil said that he foresaw that the Zionists, whose desires had meanwhile grown greatly, were not likely to be satisfied with what the British found it possible to do for them.[5]

The motives that led to the issue of the Balfour Declaration were, as is the rule when similar momentous political steps are taken, mixed. Allusion has already been made to the desire to secure for the British cause

[1] *The Arab Awakening*, p. 268.
[2] March 23, 1918.
[3] *The Letters of T. E. Lawrence*, p. 269.
[4] *The Truth about the Peace Treaties*, by D. Lloyd George, p. 1143.
[5] *idem*, p. 1150.

THE BALFOUR DECLARATION

the sympathies of the Jews of other lands, in particular those of the United States of America, and of Russia. Hardly less effective was the traditional sympathy of the British with the Jews, shown on a hundred occasions in the past, an interest, fed on the Bible for generations, in Palestine and the Jewish connexion, past and future, with that country. There was also probably another motive, an imperial and strategic one. To say that the control of the Suez Canal is one of the paramount British imperial interests is a truism. To assure that control was one of the reasons for the British occupation of Egypt. The other flank of the Canal was protected by a desert and behind it an Ottoman province from which, it was assumed, no danger could come. The events of the War still being fought had shown that this latter assumption was not altogether correct and that danger might come from Palestine. In any event the end of the War would bring to the front the disposal of the non-Turkish lands of the Ottoman Empire, of which Palestine was one. Very probably the country would obtain a new master, one not necessarily friendly and even if not unfriendly, no longer, like Turkey, militarily insignificant. It thus became almost a British interest that Palestine should come under British control. Such a desideratum brought the British and the Zionists together, for the latter knew that they could not stand without British support and that it was only under the shelter of the British flag that the Jewish experiment in Palestine could possibly succeed.

One other suggestion has been made of the reason for the issue of the Balfour Declaration and for the expression of sympathy and promises of assistance that it contained. The most distinguished of the exponents of this view was the Prime Minister of the time. One feels however that in this instance Mr. Lloyd George has given rein to his wonderful imagination, for there can be no shadow of a basis for it. That the suggestion was made thoughtlessly is evident, for if it be examined it will be found that it reflects favourably on neither of the supposed parties—the British Government that issued the Declaration, and the Zionists who accepted it. The suggestion is that the Declaration was given to Dr. Weizmann in return for the support of the Allied cause by the Jews of the world. In the first place Dr. Weizmann neither had nor claimed to have the power to commit the Jews of the world or any section of them except perhaps the relatively insignificant body of organized Zionists and even of these he was still only the self-appointed spokesman. Secondly the sympathy and support of the Jews of the British Empire and the Allied states were already wholeheartedly with their own governments and need not be purchased. As for the Jews of Germany and her allies, they were loyal German and Austrian citizens, as wholeheartedly loyal as were the British and French Jews to their governments. They were not for sale and any attempt to purchase their support would have been bitterly resented and would have resulted only in a still more devoted loyalty. There remained the Jews of the neutral countries where opinion was more free and the expression of predilections permitted. In these countries there were both pro-German and pro-British Jews, the latter being in a majority in view of the long tradition of Jewish friendliness towards Britain and British ideals, founded on gratitude, perhaps on gratitude for favours to come. But the Jews of the neutral states also were not for sale.

THE BALFOUR DECLARATION

They also were loyal to their own governments and if their governments considered it to their interest to preserve their neutrality, their Jewish citizens were quite prepared to support them in that. The suggestions that the Balfour Declaration was given in payment for the support of the Jews of the world belongs to the category of anti-Semitic fairy tales from which Jewry has suffered for so long and continues to suffer.[1] Dr. Weizmann has himself denied that the Balfour Declaration was payment for Jewish influence in America to induce the United States Government to enter the War. He gave it a far higher and moral motive, 'recognition of the yearning of an old race' and a desire to redress the unhappy situation of so many Jews in Europe. He disclaimed also the suggestion that the motive was in any way an imperialistic one, pointing out that 'when the British Government agreed to issue the famous Balfour Declaration, it agreed on one condition: that Palestine should not be the charge of Great Britain'.[2]

Finally to return to the interpretation of the Balfour Declaration offered by the Zionists in London, who had discussed it line by line and word by word with the representatives of the British Government, who had done their utmost to secure changes in the wording in some respects and had both succeeded and failed in their efforts, and who were for those reasons unquestioned authorities on the real meaning of the Declaration, no more authoritative version can be given than that of the clearest minded and wisest of them all.

---

[1] See in particular Mr. Lloyd George's speech in the House of Commons on 19 June 1936 and his broadcast address on 23 May 1939.

[2] 'Palestine To-day' in *International Affairs*, Sept.-Oct., 1936, p. 673.

108   PALESTINE: A POLICY

Ahad Ha'Am, who was kept acquainted step by step with all the turns in the controversy, has left a statement of what he understood the Balfour Declaration to mean.

'"To facilitate the establishment in Palestine of a National Home for the Jewish People"—that is the text of the promise given to us by the British Government. But that is not the text suggested to the Government by the Zionist spokesmen. They wished it to read: "the reconstitution of Palestine as the National Home of the Jewish People"; but when the happy day arrived on which the Declaration was signed and sealed by the Government, it was found to contain the first formula and not the second. That is to say, the allusion to the fact that we are about to *re*build our *old* national home was dropped, and at the same time the words "constitution of Palestine as the national home" were replaced by "establishment of a national home in Palestine". There were some who understood at once that this had some significance; but others thought that the difference was merely one of form. Hence they sometimes attempted on subsequent occasions, when the negotiations with the Government afforded an opportunity, to formulate the promise in their own wording, as though it had not been changed. But every time they found in the Government's reply a repetition of the actual text of the Declaration—which proves that it is not a case where the same thing may be put equally well in either of two ways, but that the promise is really defined in this particular form of words, and goes no further.

'It can scarcely be necessary to explain at length

the difference between the two versions. Had the British Government accepted the version suggested to it—that Palestine should be reconstituted as the national home of the Jewish people—its promise might have been interpreted as meaning that Palestine, inhabited as it now is, was restored to the Jewish people on the ground of its historic right; that the Jewish people was to rebuild its waste places and was destined to rule over it and to manage all its affairs in its own way, without regard to the consent or non-consent of its present inhabitants. For this rebuilding (it might have been understood) is only a renewal of the ancient right of the Jews, which overrides the right of the present inhabitants, who have wrongly established their national home on a land not their own. But the British Government, as it stated expressly in the Declaration itself, was not willing to promise anything which would harm the present inhabitants of Palestine, and therefore it changed the Zionist formula, and gave it a more restricted form. The Government thinks, it would seem, that when a people has only the moral force of its claim to build its national home in a land at present inhabited by others, and has not behind it a powerful army or fleet to prove the justice of its claim, that people can have only what its right allows it in truth and justice, and not what conquering peoples take for themselves by armed force, under the cover of various "rights" invented for the occasion. Now the historic right of a people in relation to a country inhabited by others can mean only the right to settle once more in its ancestral land, to work the land and to develop its resources without hindrance. And if the inhabitants complain that strangers have come to exploit the land and its population, the historic right has a complete answer to them: these newcomers are not strangers, but the descendants of the old masters of the country, and as soon as they settle in it again, they are as good as natives. And not only the settlers as individuals, but the collective body as a people, when it has once more put into this country a part of its national wealth—men, capital, cultural institutions and so forth—has again in the country its national home, and has the right to extend and complete its home up to the limit of its capacity. But this historic right does not over-ride the right of the other inhabitants, which is a tangible right based on generation after generation of life and work in the country. The country is at present their national home too, and they too have the right to develop their national potentialities so far as they are able. This position, then, makes Palestine common ground for different peoples, each of which tries to establish its national home there; and in this position it is impossible for the national home of either of them to be complete and to embrace all that is involved in the conception of a "national home". If you build your house not on untenanted ground, but in a place where there are other inhabited houses, you are sole master only as far as your front gate. Within you may arrange your effects as you please, but beyond the gate all the inhabitants are partners, and the general administration must be ordered in conformity with the good of all of them. Similarly, national homes of different peoples in the same country can demand only national freedom for each one in its internal affairs, and the affairs of the country which are common to all of them are administered by all the "householders" jointly if the relations between them and their degree of development qualify them for the task, or, if that condition is not yet fulfilled, by a guardian from outside, who takes care that the rights of none shall be infringed.

'When, then, the British Government promised to facilitate the establishment *in Palestine of a national home* for the Jewish people—and not, as was suggested to it, the reconstruction of Palestine as the national home of the Jewish people—that promise meant two things. It meant in the first place recognition of the historic right of the Jewish people to build its national home in Palestine, with a promise of assistance from the British Government; and it meant in the second place a negation of the power of that right to over-ride the right of the present inhabitants and to make the Jewish people sole ruler in the country. The national home of the Jewish people must be built out of the free material which can still be found in the country itself, and out of that which the Jews will bring in from outside or will create by their work, without overthrowing the national home of the other inhabitants. And as the two homes are contiguous, and friction and conflicts of interest are inevitable, especially in the early period of the building of the Jewish national home, of which not even the foundations have yet been properly laid, the promise necessarily demands, though it is not expressly so stated, that a guardian shall be appointed over the two homes—that is, over the whole country —to see to it that the owner of the historic right, while he does not injure the inhabitants in their internal affairs, shall not on his side have obstacles put in his way by his neighbour, who at present is stronger than he. And in course of time, when the new national home is fully built, and its tenant is able to rely, no less than his neighbour, on the right which belongs to a large population living and working in the country, it will be possible to raise the question whether the time has not come to hand over the control of the country to the "householders" themselves, so that they may together administer their joint affairs, fairly and justly, in accordance with the needs of each of them and the value of his work for the revival and development of the country.

'This and no more, it seems to me, is what we can find in the Balfour Declaration; and this and no more is what our leaders and writers ought to have told the people, so that it should not imagine more than what is actually there, and afterwards relapse into despair and absolute scepticism.'[1]

This was written in June 1920. Twenty years later Ahad Ha'Am's influence with British statesmen seems to have been greater than that with Zionist leaders.

As for the English non-Zionists, speaking on behalf also of the parallel classes in American and West European Jewry, they issued a 'statement of policy' in which they approved the Balfour Declaration, 'it being understood that nothing in that letter shall be

[1] 'In 1921 Mr. Churchill, then Colonial Secretary, confirmed this view in two sentences when addressing an influential Arab deputation in Palestine. 'The establishment of a national home does not mean a Jewish government to dominate the Arabs. . . . We cannot tolerate the expropriation of one set of people by another.'

held to imply that Jews constitute a separate political nationality all over the world or that Jewish citizens of countries outside Palestine owe political allegiance to the Government of that country'. This statement was adopted by the Joint Foreign Committee in February 1919, in preparation for the Peace Conference, fourteen months after the issue of the Balfour Declaration. In those fourteen months the British non-Zionists or anti-Zionists had advanced, for in the Statement they urged 'that the political, economic and moral organization of the country be such as to facilitate the increase and self-government of the Jewish population with a view to its eventual predominance in the government of the state, in accordance with the principles of democracy . . . that there shall be the fullest equality of political and economic rights for the members of all races and religious communities', that Hebrew shall be an official language of Palestine and the Jewish sabbath and holy days official days of rest for the Jewish citizens and that the education of Jewish children, on a Hebrew basis, shall be entrusted to the central authority of the Jewish population. Zionism having been adopted as an article of British policy, the British Jews felt it to be a matter of their British loyalty to put aside any misgivings they might still have and to support it.

CHAPTER VII

ZIONISM IN PRACTICE

The Zionist Organisation: The Jewish Agency: Early Misfortunes: The War in Palestine: The Resumption of Immigration: The Jewish Development.

AS HAS already been stated, the Zionist Organization was formed at Basle at the first Zionist Congress in August 1897. Its purpose was to be the instrument whereby the goal of Zionism, the fulfilment of the Basle Programme, was to be attained. Its beginnings were naturally small. The Organisation was originally built up of members who paid the 'shekel', an annual registration fee, at first a franc or its equivalent, now a small sum varying in different countries. Election to the biennial congresses is still by the shekel-payers who should be limited to Jews and Jewesses of eighteen years and upwards, no shekel-payer to have more than one vote. Elections are as a rule conducted separately in the different countries, lists or tickets nominated by the various parties within the Movement being voted for. The surplus votes go to the international list of the party. Zionists in different countries soon became organized in national groups or federations of societies. In some cases the grouping was not national but was based on some other community of views. For instance there is in England, outside of the Zionist

Federation of Great Britain and Ireland, the Order of Ancient Maccabaeans, a friendly society limited in its membership to Zionists. There is also the Women's International Zionist Organization with constituent societies in several countries and also the Hadassah Organization, a similar but independent organization of American Jewish women. Religiously observant Zionists have grouped themselves together in the Mizrachi Organization, whose members however vote as ordinary Zionists. The Socialist party in Zionism also has its own organization and so have the less important other parties. There is apparently no hindrance to a man being a member of more than one organization. All these parties and organizations, through their members, elect their representatives to the Congress every second year. The electorate is, however, much larger than the combined membership of the societies, for many unaffiliated Jews buy the shekel and thus secure a vote. In a world-wide electorate, scattered among peoples whose political and administrative education is at all stages of development, electoral irregularities are inevitable and Zionists are necessarily no exception to the general rule. There is reason to believe that there are many cases of plural voting and it is also probable that sometimes all the members of a family, no matter how young, buy the shekel and vote. However, these irregularities are of little practical consequence since many, of late most, of the elections to Congress are unopposed.

The Congress elects a president who is for the most part decorative—the office is one of honour more than anything else, a Zionist peerage—and an executive under a chairman. It is with this executive that the direction of the Organisation and its policy rest between any two Congresses. To these Congresses the Executive has to report and is responsible. In theory the Executive is also under the control of the Council which is supposed to meet at intervals of six months, but in practice meets less frequently and has little influence over it. Even the Congress is largely powerless where the Executive is concerned, the continental method of conducting business playing into the hands of those in office. Moreover the Congress invariably exceeds the period appointed for its deliberations and in the rush and turmoil of its last hours when the resolutions are voted on in a batch, the proceedings are always weighted in favour of those in office. Thus although there have been frequent changes of personnel among the less important members of the Executive, from the Congress of 1921 which first gave him constitutional office until to-day, the Zionist Organisation has always been in the hands of Weizmann. Even during the interlude of 1931 to 1935, when Sokolow occupied his place, the power still remained in effect with him and the party —the Zionist-Socialists—on which he grew more and more to lean.

At first the Zionist Organisation was purely a political and propagandist body with no administrative or colonization functions. Its income was small and its needs not much larger. Practical Zionism, in contradistinction from the political variety, was, however, never completely suppressed, and for the furtherance of any programme the 'Practical Zionists' might adopt, no matter how small it might be, money was necessary. The income from the shekel never left a surplus after the expenses of administration had been paid. In fact it was seldom adequate for this purpose, and the difference had to be made up out of the private pockets of Herzl and other relatively wealthy supporters. Relatively is used advisedly, for not until very recent days has the Zionist Organisation ever attracted any Jew who can be termed wealthy. To meet this new need the Jewish National Fund was founded in 1901. Its purpose was the acquisition and development of land in Palestine which should be the inalienable property of the Jewish people. This land therefore is never sold. It is let on long renewable leases to Jewish settlers in Palestine, when situated in towns as a rule to Jewish institutions. Until the end of 1940 over five million pounds had in all been collected by the Jewish National Fund and 515,950 dunams (nearly 130,000 acres) purchased by it in Palestine. There is one other principal fund of the Zionist Organisation: the *Keren Hayesod* which was founded in 1920. This fund is responsible for all the expenditure of the Zionist Organisation, apart from the purchase and development of land and the cost of the administration of the Organisation. It subventions Jewish education and health services in Palestine. It pays all the cost of immigration, from the selection of the immigrants until their absorption into industry or agriculture. It is responsible for the maintenance of unemployed immigrants, invests money in industrial undertakings and helps in innumerable other ways in supporting the *Yishub*, the Jewish community of Palestine. The total sum collected by the *Keren Hayesod* until the end of 1940 was £7,950,000. The *Keren Hayesod* was originally intended to be outside the Zionist Organisation, to be a Jewish as distinct from a Zionist undertaking. It is true that much of its income is derived from people who are not formal Zionists, but in effect the *Keren Hayesod* is and always has been a part of the Zionist Organisation and is controlled and directed by it.

There was a third financial institution that was founded by the Zionist Organisation. This was the Jewish Colonial Trust, established in 1899 with a nominal capital of two million pounds although less than £400,000 has been raised even after nearly forty years of effort. The only apparent result of the existence of this Trust was the birth of a daughter, the Anglo-Palestine Bank, which is the bank of the Zionist Organisation, of the greater part of Palestine Jewry and of a number of Jews in England. It is an English company. The Anglo-Palestine Bank has in effect long ago absorbed its parent.

The headquarters of the Zionist Organisation, previously in Vienna, Cologne and Berlin successively, was removed to London after the War of 1914. After the confirmation of the Mandate and the apparent stabilization of the situation in Palestine, the departments of the Organisation which had by now become a sort of small government office, were transferred one by one to Palestine, where they now all are, except a political department in London which is in effect little more than the Chairman's personal office. The Zionist Executive also inevitably separated into two parts, the Chairman and one other member concerned solely with political matters remaining in London, the other departments, including a political one, being stationed in Jerusalem. The Executive Committee through one or other of its parts is in close contact with

ZIONISM IN PRACTICE

the Colonial Office and the British Government in London and with the Palestine Government in Jerusalem.

In the meanwhile, in the year 1929, the Zionist Organisation underwent a change in title. This is the only practical effect of a step taken on the 14th of August of that year, although the Organisation still exists and under its old name. The Mandate for Palestine laid down in Article 4 that 'an appropriate Jewish Agency shall be recognized as a public body for the purpose of advising and co-operating with the Administration of Palestine' and 'The Zionist Organisation, so long as its organisation and constitution are in the opinion of the Mandatory appropriate, shall be recognized as such Agency'. It was always the intention or hope of the British Government that the Palestine experiment should be conducted in co-operation not with any party in Jewry, even one so important and enthusiastic as the Zionists, but with Jewry as a whole, and Dr. Weizmann certainly shared this view. But among his followers there were many that fell far below him in stature and were perhaps not unnaturally anxious, having borne the brunt of the battle for more than a generation, in the hour of apparent victory, to keep to themselves all of its fruits. The non-Zionists or anti-Zionists also had loyally accepted the result of the struggle for the new status in Palestine, even though they still felt many misgivings, and had stood aside, refraining from creating any difficulties for those upon whom the burden of conducting the experiment rested. But this abstinence by them was not intended to be more than a sort of benevolent neutrality. It did not mean that they intended to join with the Zionists in putting into effect a policy with which they were not wholly in sympathy or of whose practicability they were not convinced. So far as his followers were concerned Dr. Weizmann ultimately had his way. With the non-Zionists, or at any rate a substantial and influential section of them, he also succeeded, but only after five years of negotiation. It was at the Zionist Congress of August 1929 that he managed, against considerable opposition, to get his agreement with the non-Zionists ratified. By this agreement the Zionist Organisation, while retaining its identity and existence, was to transfer to a new body, a Jewish Agency, consisting as to one half of the Zionist Organisation and the other of members of bodies, more or less representative of the Jewish communities in the principal countries of the world, its functions in Palestine and Britain.

The constitution, like most if not all political instruments, was a compromise. The non-Zionists after much hesitation agreed to a monopoly for Jewish labour on Jewish Agency undertakings. '(e) The Agency shall promote agricultural colonization based on Jewish labour, and in all works and undertakings carried out or furthered by the Agency it shall be deemed to be a matter of principle that Jewish labour shall be employed.' On the other hand, in the words of Felix Warburg, one of the non-Zionist architects of the Agency, 'the non-Zionists always understood that the Jewish state idea would not be pursued by the Jewish Agency.' They recognized that it rendered agreement with the Arabs impossible and without such an agreement there was no hope for the future of the Jews in Palestine.

The new Jewish Agency, however, perhaps never had an opportunity for a real existence. It was from its birth nothing more than a shadow or a veil. Contem-

ZIONISM IN PRACTICE

poraneous with its appearance was a violent anti-Jewish outbreak by the Arabs of Palestine, influenced to some extent, it was claimed, by the fears aroused by this new Jewish co-operation which appeared to be replete with further threats to the Arab position. Within a few days of the creation of the Agency its main architect with Weizmann, Louis Marshall, the universally accepted head of American Jewry, a non-Zionist of keen vision and wide sympathies, died after a very brief illness. Shortly afterwards the other great pillar of the Agency, Lord Melchett, who although never a member of the Zionist Organisation had developed from being a non-Jew, albeit a 'non-Aryan', with no interest whatsoever in Jewish affairs, into a philo-Zionist and a passionate supporter of Jewish settlement in Palestine, also died. A further blow was the catastrophic economic depression which was gradually spreading throughout the world, engulfing even the United States of America, the land of supposed endless prosperity. By this much of the material wealth on which the Jewish Agency hoped for its support disappeared. But not the least among the wounds by which the new Agency was incapacitated was the peculiar definition of 'non-Zionist', a Jew who did not at the moment hold Zionist office. By applying this definition the governing body and administration, which were supposed to be half Zionist and half non-Zionist, were in effect almost entirely Zionists.[1] The few genuine non-Zionists who

[1] With the retirement of Dr. Maurice Hexter in 1939 the personnel of the Executive of the Jewish Agency consisted solely of Zionists, some still in office, others formerly there. The Zionization of the personnel proceeded so far that in February 1940 a manifesto of the 'Zionist Executive' was signed by among others a 'non-Zionist' member of the Jewish Agency Executive, Dr. A. Ruppin, described for the occasion as 'Member of the Zionist Executive.'

found themselves in this unexpected and not altogether congenial milieu inevitably lost interest, and the Jewish Agency and its instruments quickly became merely the Zionist Organisation under a new name. The Zionists had overleapt their sell and if they had ever wanted non-Zionist co-operation they had sacrificed it in reaching for too much. The non-Zionists, on their part never very enthusiastic, who should nevertheless have thrown all their weight into keeping the Agency on the lines which in their opinion were the ones to lead to success, were at the best passive.

However politics, even internal politics, are not everything and while the manœuvres for the control of the Organisation and the securing of funds for its work went on, the work in Palestine, the real purpose behind everything, continued without interruption. When the War broke out in 1914 there were forty-four Jewish agricultural settlements in Palestine, all small, with a total population of about 12,000. Tel Aviv, now a town of about 139,000 inhabitants, was then but a suburb of Jaffa on which it was dependent in all respects. During the War there was no advance. In fact there was retrogression. The Jews of the villages clung to the land and lived on its produce. The only exceptions were those who found themselves between the opposing armies and they had perforce to leave their homes which were in most cases destroyed. With the Jews of the towns it was otherwise. A large proportion were Allied subjects, Russians, and of these many were permitted by the Turks to go to Egypt. The Jewish town population was to a large extent dependent on foreign charity or on support by friends and relatives abroad. Funds from Russia, their principal source,

ZIONISM IN PRACTICE

and, to a less extent, from Britain were no longer available. As a consequence many previously dependent on these means of existence died of starvation. To some extent the gap was filled by American generosity, but this was not sufficient. As a result a Jewish population of about a hundred thousand in the early summer of 1914 was reduced by death and exile to less than sixty thousand. In advance of the approach of the British army Tel Aviv was compulsorily evacuated by the Turks and some of its inhabitants taken as far as Northern Syria and Asia Minor.

The end of the War, even the occupation of Southern Palestine, gave a great encouragement to Jewish settlement. While the military were still in control and the country nominally closed to new immigration, the exiles began to return from Egypt and more distant countries and among them was an appreciable mixture of newcomers, for the most part from Russia and Poland, then in a state of revolution and upheaval. The change from a military to a civil administration brought with it the removal of the nominal ban on immigration and land purchase. In the first months of the new régime Jewish immigration was in effect unlimited except by the Zionist Organisation alone. This Organisation was, however, unable to take full advantage of its opportunity. The rising hostility and fear of the Arabs also quickly boiled over and within eight months the opportunity had passed and the control of immigration was taken into the hands of the Government where it has since remained, despite numerous Zionist protests. However, this did not by any means mean the cessation of immigration or even its diminution. It meant the exercise of greater responsibility in the selection of immigrants and an attempt at correlating their number to the absorptive capacity of the country. At the beginning of June 1921, after the closing of the gates of the country for five weeks, immigration was resumed with the introduction of a system of categories which, although amended in detail from time to time, is still the basis of the existing legislation.

Immigration was however not sufficient. Employment had to be provided for the immigrants after arrival. The largest, almost the only, employer was then the Government, especially if this term is taken to include the military authorities. There were many public works in hand and projected in the first years of Lord Samuel's administration. Jewish labour was for the most part inexperienced in such trades as building and road-making to which the demand was almost limited, but the Government and its officials were very patient and sympathetic. Otherwise the first months of the post-war period would have been marked by a grave crisis. Later the Zionists and other friends established industries, entered into a building programme of their own, especially with regard to houses of which there was a great scarcity, and also began to found new agricultural villages. The course of development, industrial and agricultural, has continued without a break, the flow of funds for the purpose—in recent years, in many cases brought by settlers themselves—rising and falling but always continuing. As a consequence an estimated Jewish population on 1 July 1920, the day of the introduction of the Civil Administration, of about 66,000 has grown to 463,535 (31 December 1940) of which 327,385 represents the number of Jewish immigrants. From this figure the number of those who have abandoned the undertaking and left the country and also of native-born emigrants should be deducted, but on the other hand an unknown number of illegal immigrants, those who have entered the country by evading the passport controls, must be added. At the same time the number of Jewish villages has grown to about 240, several of the small country towns rather than villages, with a population of 110,000. Tel Aviv, in 1920 a suburb of Jaffa with a population of a couple of thousand, is now the largest town in Palestine with about 139,000 inhabitants, all, with the exception of 300 or 400 domestic servants with a sprinkling of Government officials, Jews. There has also during the past twenty years been a remarkable Jewish cultural development in Palestine. Hebrew was at once on the institution of the civil régime raised to the dignity of an official language. The Hebrew school system, culminating in a university, is completely in the hands of the Jewish community, the Government contributing a grant on a capitation basis. There is a large number of Hebrew newspapers and printing presses, Hebrew theatres, one company with an international reputation, an orchestra of outstanding merit recruited from executants attached in happier days to the most famous of those of Central Europe, and many other musical organizations.

CHAPTER VIII

THE MANDATE AND ITS INTERPRETATION

The Terms of the Mandate: Need for Interpretation: The Churchill White Paper: Its Interpretation: The 1929 Outbreak: The Shaw Commission: The Passfield White Paper and the Macdonald Letter: Sir Arthur Wauchope's Régime: A Legislative Council.

THE TERMS of the Mandate for Palestine were approved by the Council of the League of Nations on 24 July 1922, after some two years of discussion and delay, and proclaimed on 11 September. The Mandate, however, did not enter officially into force until 29 September 1923. The delay was in part due to the desire of the French Government that the Mandates for Palestine and Syria should be approved simultaneously and to the difficulties raised by the Italian Government in the way of the latter. The Government of the United States, also, although it declined to be a party to the new system that had brought the mandates into existence and refused to accept any liability or duty under that system, demanded equality under the Mandates with the Powers on whom the maintenance of the new European system rested. A settlement with the United States was also reached and that difficulty removed.

The Preamble and clauses of the Mandate for

Palestine that concerned specifically the position of the Jews there run as follows:

'Whereas the Principal Allied Powers have also agreed that the Mandatory should be responsible for putting into effect the declaration originally made on November 2, 1917, by the Government of His Britannic Majesty, and adopted by the said Powers, in favour of the establishment in Palestine of a national home for the Jewish people, it being clearly understood that nothing should be done which might prejudice the civil and religious rights of existing non-Jewish communities in Palestine, or the rights and political status enjoyed by Jews in any other country; and

'Whereas recognition has thereby been given to the historical connexion of the Jewish people with Palestine and to the grounds for reconstituting their national home in that country. . . .

'Article 2. The Mandatory shall be responsible for placing the country under such political, administrative and economic conditions as will secure the establishment of the Jewish national home, as laid down in the preamble, and the development of self-governing institutions, and also for safeguarding the civil and religious rights of all the inhabitants of Palestine, irrespective of race and religion.

'Article 4. An appropriate Jewish agency shall be recognized as a public body for the purpose of advising and co-operating with the Administration of Palestine in such economic, social and other matters as may affect the establishment of the Jewish national home and the interests of the Jewish population in Palestine and, subject always to the control of the

Administration, to assist and take part in the development of the country.

'The Zionist Organization, so long as its organization and constitution are in the opinion of the Mandatory appropriate, shall be recognized as such agency. It shall take steps in consultation with His Britannic Majesty's Government to secure the co-operation of all Jews who are willing to assist in the establishment of the Jewish national home.

'Article 6. The Administration of Palestine, while ensuring that the rights and position of other sections of the population are not prejudiced, shall facilitate Jewish immigration under suitable conditions and shall encourage in co-operation with the Jewish agency, referred to in Article 4 close settlement by Jews on the land, including State lands and waste lands not required for public purposes.

'Article 7. The Administration of Palestine shall be responsible for enacting a nationality law. There shall be included in this law provisions framed so as to facilitate the acquisition of Palestinian citizenship by Jews who take up their permanent residence in Palestine.

'Article 11. . . . The Administration may arrange with the Jewish Agency mentioned in Article 4 to construct or operate, upon fair and equitable terms, any public works, services and utilities, and to develop any of the natural resources of the country, in so far as these matters are not indirectly undertaken by the Administration. Any such arrangements shall provide that no profits distributed by such agency, directly or indirectly, shall exceed a reasonable rate of interest on the capital, and any further profits

THE MANDATE AND ITS INTERPRETATION

shall be utilized by it for the benefit of the country in a manner approved by the Administration.

'Article 22. English, Arabic and Hebrew shall be the official languages of Palestine. Any statement or inscription in Arabic on stamps or money in Palestine shall be repeated in Hebrew and any statement or inscription in Hebrew shall be repeated in Arabic.

The Preamble in effect incorporated the terms of the Balfour Declaration, but in the second paragraph quoted went somewhat beyond them. Attention has been called in an earlier chapter to the discussions and differences that arose over the alternatives 'the establishment in Palestine of a national home for the Jewish people' and 'the reconstitution of Palestine as the National Home of the Jewish People.' Despite the pressure of the Zionists the former was accepted for the Declaration, but both alternatives appear in the Preamble to the Mandate. It looked as if the latter had slipped in by accident as a result of the Zionist persistence. However the terms of the Mandate were still far less in accordance with the extreme Zionist demands which had grown rapidly since the talks that culminated in the Balfour Declaration. In the intervening period the politically immature and unrealistic Jewish masses of Eastern Europe had entered the discussions. In America also the wisest Jewish statesmen of the calibre of Justice Louis Brandeis had been replaced by others of a more excitable and chauvinistic disposition. As early as 1919 many of the most prominent Zionists began to travel away from their old ideals into more stormy and inadequately charted seas. Dr. Weizmann himself, the disciple of Ahad Ha'Am, before the Peace Conference on 27 February used the unfortunate phrase that he looked forward to a Palestine 'as Jewish as England is English or America American' and to show that this view was not a mere *obiter dictum* he repeated it in interviews published in *The Times* and *The New York Times* on the following day. In the Diaspora as well as in Palestine the delay of two years had brought difficulties and trouble.

The extreme Zionist demands which were rejected before the terms of the Mandate were approved included the recognition of the historic title of the Jewish people to Palestine and the right of the Jews to reconstitute Palestine as their National Home, the development of a self-governing Jewish commonwealth and the right of the Jewish Agency to undertake public works and receive concessions provided the Administration did not propose to undertake them itself. In the meanwhile all Jews settled or to settle in the country were to be automatically naturalized. The Zionists consequently received far less than their desires. However they were always willing to guarantee, after their ambitions had been attained—in this following the Balfour Declaration— the civil and religious rights of the non-Jewish inhabitants.

The Mandate in effect superseded the Balfour Declaration, of which it was not only an elaboration, but also to some extent an interpretation. It also had behind it a far greater moral and legal force. The Declaration, the Hogarth Message and the many other earlier pronouncements remained legally merely of academic interest. The Mandate, however, also suffered to some extent from lack of definition and since the Arabs of

THE MANDATE AND ITS INTERPRETATION

Palestine were as little inclined to accept it as they were the Balfour Declaration and took steps, both constitutional and criminal, to secure its annulment, some further definition, if not modification, soon became urgently necessary. Before the Mandate had been formally adopted there were two outbreaks which, whatever their immediate causes, developed into violent and widespread attack by Arabs on their Jewish neighbours or passers-by. The earlier was at Easter 1920 when the country was still in the control of the military. It was suggested by the Zionists that there was a certain amount of sympathy on the part of the military administration or at any rate of some of its influential members with the Arabs and a consequent dilatoriness in suppressing the outbreak. As a consequence the military administration was brought to an end and replaced by a civil one under a Jewish High Commissioner, who, if not himself a Zionist, was very sympathetically disposed to Zionism as he then understood it. The change had no effect on the Arab population. If anything it made it more hostile and there was another and more deadly and widespread anti-Jewish outbreak within a few months of Sir Herbert Samuel's arrival in Palestine. It was then decided to reconsider the situation and issue a new interpretation of the Government policy. This interpretation, known as the Churchill White Paper—Mr. Winston Churchill was responsible for the document as Colonial Secretary—was accepted by the Zionist Organisation through Dr. Weizmann and the other members of the Executive of whom one was Vladimir Jabotinsky who afterwards seceded and formed a new organization on the ground that the orthodox Zionists were too amenable to British influence and were willing to accept far less than was their due, and approved by the Council of the League of Nations. It was in fact the official and accepted definition of the Mandate and so that there should be no misunderstanding it was issued simultaneously with the publication of that document.

The main points of the Churchill White Paper and of the constitution that was based on it were Jewish immigration into Palestine should be permitted, but 'This immigration cannot be so great in volume as to exceed whatever may be the economic capacity of the country at the time to absorb new arrivals. It is essential to assure that the immigrants should not be a burden on the people of Palestine as a whole, and that they should not deprive any section of the present population of their employment'. A committee of the proposed Legislative Council was to be appointed 'to confer with the Administration upon matters relating to the regulation of immigration'. In the event of a difference of opinion the decision would rest with His Majesty's Government, Furthermore any considerable section of the population of Palestine would have the right of appeal to the League of Nations. An elected Legislative Council, with advisory powers, consisting of eight Moslems, two Jews and two Christians, with the High Commissioner as chairman and ten official members,[1] should be set up, with a promise that after this Council had gained experience, its powers would be increased. As for the somewhat exaggerated claims of some Jews and the fears of the Arabs regarding the meaning of the Balfour Declaration, it was stated clearly that 'Unauthorized

[1] The primary electors qualified to vote in the projected elections numbered 135,425 Moslems, 16,703 Jews and 12,319 Christians.

statements have been made to the effect that the purpose in view is to create a wholly Jewish Palestine. Phrases have been used such as that Palestine is to become "as Jewish as England is English". His Majesty's Government regard any such expectation as impracticable and have no such aim in view. Nor have they at any time contemplated, as appears to be feared by the Arab Delegation, the disappearance or the subordination of the Arabic population, language or culture in Palestine. They would draw attention to the fact that the terms of the Declaration referred to do not contemplate that Palestine as a whole should be converted into a Jewish National Home, but that such a Home should be founded *in Palestine.* In this connexion it has been observed with satisfaction that at the meeting of the Zionist Congress, the supreme governing body of the Zionist Organisation, held at Carlsbad in September, 1921, a resolution was passed expressing as the official statement of Zionist aims "the determination of the Jewish people to live with the Arab people on terms of unity and mutual respect, and together with them to make the common home into a flourishing community, the upbuilding of which may assure to each of its peoples an undisturbed national development".

'It is also necessary to point out that the Zionist Commission in Palestine, now termed the Palestine Zionist Executive, has not desired to possess, and does not possess, any share in the general administration of the country. Nor does the special position assigned to the Zionist Organisation in Article IV of the Draft Mandate for Palestine imply any such functions. That special position relates to the measures to be taken in Palestine affecting the Jewish population, and contemplates that the Organisation may assist in the general development of the country, but does not entitle it to share in any degree in its government.

'Further, it is contemplated that the status of all citizens of Palestine in the eyes of the law shall be Palestinian, and it has never been intended that they, or any section of them, should possess any other juridical status. . . .

'. . . When it is asked what is meant by the development of the Jewish National Home in Palestine, it may be answered that it is not the imposition of a Jewish nationality upon the inhabitants of Palestine as a whole, but the further development of the existing Jewish community, with the assistance of Jews in other parts of the world, in order that it may become a centre in which the Jewish people as a whole may take, on grounds of religion and race, an interest and a pride. But in order that this community should have the best prospect of free development and provide a full opportunity for the Jewish people to display its capacities, it is essential that it should know that it is in Palestine as of right and not on sufferance. That is the reason why it is necessary that the existence of a Jewish National Home in Palestine should be internationally guaranteed, and that it should be formally recognized to rest upon ancient historic connexion.'

At the same time and by a separate document, Palestine east of the Jordan and the Dead Sea (Transjordan) was excluded from the jurisdiction of those articles of the Mandate that relate to the Jewish National Home. There was a dispute between the British Government and the Arab spokesmen whether in the treaty with Hussein, then Sherif of Mecca, Western Palestine was

THE MANDATE AND ITS INTERPRETATION 135

or was not excluded from the territories which at the end of the War should be placed under Arab control. The British Government had, however, never suggested that Eastern Palestine (Transjordan) should be so excluded.

The Zionist Organisation on receipt of the terms of the proposed constitution resolved 'The Executive of the Zionist Organisation, having taken note of the statement relative to British policy in Palestine, transmitted to them by the Colonial Office under date June 3rd, 1922, assure His Majesty's Government that the activities of the Zionist Organisation will be conducted in conformity with the policy therein set forth.' The Arab Delegation, then in London, rejected the proposals. They demanded in effect the repeal of the Balfour Declaration, the institution of national self-government and the withdrawal from the Jewish Agency of its privileges. They were careful to differentiate between the pre-War Jewish population who 'never had any trouble with their Arab neighbours' and were in no respect responsible for the Balfour Declaration, and the Zionists, both those who had settled in Palestine and those still in the Diaspora, who were strongly suspected of political designs on the country.

The new policy was summarized by the Government in a telegraphic dispatch to the High Commissioner sent on 29 June:

'A White Paper will be laid on Saturday the 1st July covering correspondence between His Majesty's Government and Palestine Arab Delegation and Zionist Organisation from 21st February to 23rd June 1922. This correspondence includes official statement of British policy on Palestine of which summary follows:

'(1) His Majesty's Government re-affirm Declaration of November, 1917 which is not susceptible of change.

'(2) A Jewish National Home will be founded in Palestine. The Jewish people will be in Palestine as of right and not on sufferance. But His Majesty's Government have no such aim in view as that Palestine should become as Jewish as England is English.

'(3) Nor do His Majesty's Government contemplate disappearance or subordination of Arab population, language or culture.

'(4) Status of all citizens of Palestine will be Palestinian. No section of population will have any other status in the eyes of the law.

'(5) His Majesty's Government intend to foster establishment of full measure of self-government in Palestine, and as the next step a Legislative Council with a majority of elected members will be set up immediately.

'(6) Special position of Zionist Executive does not entitle it to share in any degree in government of country.

'(7) Immigration will not exceed economic capacity of the country at the time to absorb new arrivals.

'(8) Committee of elected members of Legislative Council will confer with Administration upon matters relating to regulation of immigration. Any difference of opinion will be referred to His Majesty's Government.

'(9) Any religious community or considerable section of population claiming that terms of mandate are not being fulfilled will have right of appeal to League of Nations.

'The Executive of Zionist Organisation have formally assured His Majesty's Government that the activities of Zionist Organisation will be conducted in conformity with policy set forth in statement.'

This policy of the Lloyd George-Churchill Government, which although looked at askance by the Zionists had been accepted by them, was repeatedly confirmed by successive British Governments, in October 1923 (Baldwin, Prime Minister and Duke of Devonshire, Colonial Secretary), June 1924 (Ramsay Macdonald and J. H. Thomas), April 1925 (Baldwin and Amery), and April and October 1930 (Ramsay Macdonald and Lord Passfield).

The earlier system whereby the selection of immigrants and in effect the decision as to their numbers had been left to the Zionist Organisation had, as has been mentioned, quickly broken down and a substitute was necessary. This substitute did not entirely follow the lines laid down in the Churchill White Paper. It was only in part dependent on the 'economic absorptive capacity' of the country. This criterion was applied, in theory at any rate, so far as the immigration of labour was concerned, but the number of immigrants in other categories was unlimited so long as certain conditions were fulfilled. The other definite proposal, the formation of a legislative council and with it an Immigration

Advisory Committee, failed in view of the opposition of the Arab population. The primary elections[1] were held and the Jews voted in full force, but except in a few localities, the Arabs abstained. The elections were thereupon cancelled. Sir Herbert Samuel, on taking office, had nominated an Advisory Council of British officials and Moslems, Jews and Christians which had lapsed when the election of a legislative council was projected. On the failure of the elections he proposed to return to the Advisory Council but the Arabs declined also to participate in this, and the High Commissioner had to be satisfied with an Advisory Council of British officials only. There was one further attempt to offer a compromise to the Arabs and that was by the institution of an Arab Agency parallel to the Jewish Agency or Zionist Organisation and with similar functions and powers. The British Government seemed to recognize that 'even though formally excluded from all share in the administration, the Jewish Agency does, in fact, by reason of its official recognition and right of access to the High Commissioner, enjoy, and thereby confer upon the Palestine Jews as a whole, a preferential position as compared with the other inhabitants of the country. To that extent it is possible to argue that existing arrangements fall short of securing complete equality between the different communities.' The offer was unanimously declined by the representatives of the Arabs of Palestine, Mr. Churchill's offer of a legislative

[1] The franchise was granted to all male Turkish subjects of twenty-five years of age and upwards who were habitually resident in Palestine on 1 September 1922, and, as a concession to the Zionists, also to all other males above the same age who stated in Palestine their intention to apply for Palestinian citizenship when the opportunity occurred and to remain permanently in the country. Palestinian citizenship had not yet been constituted.

THE MANDATE AND ITS INTERPRETATION 139

council was, however, not permanently abandoned. It was put aside to be brought out again when conditions might be more propitious.

The policy laid down in the Churchill White Paper, modified in the manner mentioned, held the field for the next fifteen years. The Advisory Council functioned without the co-operation of either Arabs or Jews. Immigration was regulated in accordance with the principles laid down, the Zionist Organisation, afterwards the Jewish Agency, being taken into consultation when the half-yearly schedules of labour immigrants were under consideration and also when any amendment of the Immigration Regulations—invariably minor ones—was contemplated. Immigration, although its numbers rose and fell, responding, with delays, to the rise and fall in the supposed prosperity of the country, continued throughout the period, so that between 1932 and 1936, 261,861 Jewish immigrants entered the country, apart from those, estimated at several thousands, who in the 'boom' years and later after the beginning of the Nazi persecution evaded the frontier controls or otherwise remained in the country without permission. In everyday life Jews and Arabs, especially in the neighbourhood of the older Jewish settlements, met on a friendly basis. Between the politicians on either side there was little contact, and politically the two elements in the population were completely separated. The Arabs persistently declined to accept the *status quo*. The Zionists on their part were also never satisfied, always demanding more, whatever they might receive. Nevertheless there seemed to be some modification in the Arab position. From time to time there arose a so-called 'Moderate' party. The Arabs like the Jews of Palestine are very prolific in the production of political parties—but it is doubtful whether the difference between the 'Moderates' and their fellow-Arabs were, although deep, ever other than personal. By 1929 the time seemed ripe for the reintroduction of Mr. Churchill's proposal for a Legislative Council. The Jews had accepted it six years earlier and presumably would not go back on that acceptance. Their number had increased greatly in the meanwhile and their representation and influence on the Council would presumably be similarly increased. The Arab leaders had given hints that they were no longer quite so intransigent on the question. Sir John Chancellor, the High Commissioner, when he went to England in the summer of that year, had therefore some justification for the hope that he would be able to preside at the birth of the long promised Legislative Council. While he was in England, however, the situation again boiled over. Incidents, trivial in themselves, increased the fears and suspicions of the Arabs. The proverbial last straw was provided and they rose in all parts of Palestine and attacked their Jewish neighbours. Sir John Chancellor hurried back to Palestine where his first action was to denounce the atrocities that had been committed by Arabs in a number of centres and to announce that the institution of a legislative council or of any other measure that might appeal to the Arabs would in the circumstances be suspended. Until the Arab leaders could control and subdue the wilder elements among their followers there could be no question of granting any concession to them.

Previous outbreaks had been mainly Arab—Moslem and Christian—Zionist. This one was both narrower and wider. The Christian Arabs for the most part remained passive, but on the other hand there was no attempt on the part of the rioters to differentiate between Zionists and other Jews, the greater number of the victims being found among the old pre-Zionist section of the population between whom and the Arabs there had never previously been any hostility. In the eyes of the Arabs all Jews were becoming Zionists. One of the not unnatural consequences of this outbreak was a boycott on the part of a large section of the Jews of all Arabs and of everything Arab. The example was quickly followed by an Arab boycott of Jews which at once spread to neighbouring lands and was on a later occasion to be developed and perfected.

The outbreak of 1929 and its causes were in due course inquired into by a commission representative of the three parties in the House of Commons under the chairmanship of Sir Walter Shaw, a retired colonial judge. This commission went very thoroughly into its work and submitted an unanimous report, except that the Labour member, Mr., now Lord, Snell, added a note of reservations in which after a mild reproof to the Palestine Administration for omissions in matters of detail, and the attribution of greater responsibility for the outbreak than his colleagues were prepared to admit, to certain prominent Arabs, he urged that the only hope for the future of Palestine was the reconciliation of Arabs and Jews. To this end he called for an authoritative Jewish pronouncement that there was no desire to drive or buy the Arabs off the land and that in all economic and social matters equality between Jew and Arab was the aim. Each race or community must concede to the other the right to live. The ideal to which the Government and all good citizens must work was a bi-racial or bi-national Palestinian State, formed of 'good Palestinian citizens of members of both races'. Mr. Snell joined with his colleagues in rejecting all the charges brought against the Palestine Government and its officers of responsibility, either active or passive, for the outbreak or the delay in suppressing it. The principal positive recommendations, on which there was unanimity, were that the Government should issue without delay a clear statement of policy including a reaffirmation of the Churchill White Paper to the effect that the Zionist Organisation was not entitled under the Mandate to share in the government of Palestine, and particulars of the course regarding immigration it intended to pursue for which it made suggestions, and that pending an agricultural survey the eviction of Arab peasant cultivators should be suspended. On the subject of constitutional development the Commission made no recommendation, but reiterated that 'the absence of any measure of self-government is greatly aggravating the difficulties of the local Administration.'

On the recommendation of the Commission Sir John Hope Simpson, who had been in charge of the successful re-settlement of the million and more Greek refugees from Turkey, was sent to Palestine to examine questions of immigration, land settlement and development. His conclusions in general confirmed those of the Shaw Commission. On the subject of immigration and land settlement he was of opinion that, taking into consideration the natural increase of the population in the next few years, the agricultural lands were already fully occupied except for those reserve lands which were the property of the Zionist Organisation. To meet the difficulty he advocated a large-scale development by the

Government of agricultural and so-called waste lands so that more land might be avaliable for cultivation and land already in occupation might be cultivated more intensively. With the Hope Simpson Report in its hands the British Government issued its new statement of policy. This was in fact little more than an elaboration of that of 1922, with the further information recently made available taken into consideration. The statement opened with a plea for co-operation between Jew and Arab and between both and the Government. The definition in the Churchill White Paper, negative as well as positive, of the position of the Jewish Agency was repeated and the determination of the Government so to administer the Mandate as to treat its pro-Jewish and pro-Arab sections of equal weight was reaffirmed. In this the Government was adopting the recently expressed opinion of the Mandates Commission of the League of Nations. The Government Statement then proceeded to lay down policy. The abortive Legislative Council proposals of 1922 were to be revived. A scheme of development as recommended by Sir John Hope Simpson would be put into effect. By this means it was hoped that opportunities for a considerable further Jewish immigration would be created and provision also made for the natural increase of the existing population, Arab and Jewish. Steps would at once be taken to safeguard the interests and welfare of existing agricultural tenants. 'The control of all disposition of land must rest with the authority in charge of the development' and transfers of land would 'be permitted only in so far as they' did 'not interfere with the plans of that authority'.[1] Jewish settlement could continue in the

[1] Cmd. 3692 of 1930.

meanwhile on the reserve lands held by Jewish agencies and immigration in accordance with the procedure already in force would also continue.

The Government announcement was received with dismay and lamentation by the Zionists. Steeped in the optimism without which their Movement would never have come into existence, they had built very high hopes on what was to come. Their disappointment was therefore all the deeper. In this disappointment they exaggerated the decisions and read into the document meanings that it did not contain. Certain unfortunate phrases in the Government White Paper also hurt and angered the Jews. The principal real offence of the new White Paper was a certain tactlessness in expression. The Arabs, although they had gained, had failed to obtain their desideratum, a National Government, and had other reasons for dissatisfaction, but were on the whole satisfied that the promise given was an improvement on the existing condition of things. When, however, the Zionists took the new policy so tragically, lamenting extravagantly as if the end of all their hopes and strivings had been reached, the Arabs were unfortunately influenced by them into reading also far more into the White Paper than it contained. There is much similarity in the psychological make-up of both Arabs and Eastern Jews. The similarity between them increases the difficulties of a mutual *modus vivendi*. The reaction, when they found that it brought them so much less than that for which the Zionists denounced it, was unfortunate. It blinded the Arabs to the virtues, from their point of view, that it contained. Thus in the end this effort by the British Government to be fair to both parties and to administer the country in the interests of both met with response

THE MANDATE AND ITS INTERPRETATION

from neither side. It was like the well-meaning man who intervenes in the quarrel of man and wife. Both forget their mutual hostility to attack the interloper.

But only temporarily. In the end none of the positive decisions of the White Paper was acted on. Although Parliament voted a Development Loan on very generous terms it was never taken up. Jewish immigration continued and after a short interval rose to undreamt-of dimensions. The purchase of land continued without restrictions. Only some not altogether effective steps were taken to safeguard the agricultural tenants in danger of removal from their holdings. The Arabs felt that all their doubts had been fully justified. Their feeling of suspicion was accentuated a few months later when the result of conversations between Dr. Weizmann, who had on the publication of the latest White Paper resigned his chairmanship of the Jewish Agency and the Zionist Organisation as a protest, and the Prime Minister and a Committee of the Cabinet was published in the form of a letter from Ramsay Macdonald, the Prime Minister, to Dr. Weizmann who expressed himself fully satisfied with the interpretations it put on the original document, and the Arab feelings were not assuaged when a little later the Zionists were again driven to a feeling akin to despair at the terms of the instructions to the newly appointed Director of Development. Unfortunately in and of Palestine even more than elsewhere there is a tendency not to read or understand documents but to accept the interpretations of parties who are more concerned in furthering their own point of view than in ascertaining or publishing the facts.

The Macdonald Letter of Dr. Weizmann, termed by the Arabs 'the Black Paper', was stated to be 'an authoritative interpretation' of the White Paper. But it had not quite an authority equal to that of the document signed by Lord Passfield, for the Prime Minister himself, speaking in the House of Commons on 11 February 1931, two days before the date of the Letter, said he was 'very unwilling to give the letter the same status as the dominating document'. The Letter, like the main document, was also largely an interpretation of the White Paper of 1922 without changing it, but its language was far less exacerbating. The Zionists, without any justification, read it as a withdrawal of the Passfield White Paper. It was certainly not that. Its object was obviously to soothe the ruffled feelings of the Zionists while disturbing as little as possible those of the Arabs. 'The words "rights and position of other sections of the population" occurring in Article 6, plainly refer to the non-Jewish community. These rights and position are not to be prejudiced, that is are not to be impaired or made worse. The effect of the policy of immigration and settlement on the economic position of the non-Jewish community cannot be excluded from consideration. But the words are not to be read as implying that existing economic conditions in Palestine should be crystallized. On the contrary, the obligation to facilitate Jewish immigration and to encourage close settlement by Jews on the land remains a positive obligation of the Mandate, and it can be fulfilled without prejudice to the rights and position of other sections of the population of Palestine.'

However, definition is of less consequence than administration. The Government of Palestine set its hand to administering the country in accordance with the new interpretation, and neither party was satisfied.

Palestinian Arabs and Jews, children of the East, had no knowledge of the virtues of compromise. As for the Zionists who had the better of the bargain, the attitude of a large party among them may be summarized in the words of Vladimir Jabotinsky, writing a year later on the subject of the Legislative Council. 'Why should we submit and try not to fight against it? It is surprising that we have not yet realized the truth that a declaration of a Minister or a High Commissioner does not yet mean a firm decision of the Government and that a firm decision by Government does not mean that it will insist on it also after a year. Further, even if Government insists upon its decision after the lapse of a year it does not mean that it would be able to execute it. There is always a great distance between the will and possibility of carrying it out.'[1]

The proposal for a Legislative Council although left long in suspense was not abandoned. Sir John Chancellor retired at the conclusion of his term of office and was succeeded by Sir Arthur Wauchope, a British general, whose administration was marked by a consistent attitude of sympathy with Zionist aspirations, without, however, showing that to be pro-Zionist one must necessarily be anti-Arab. The first four years of his term were the heyday of Zionist history in Palestine. Immigration rose threefold: the Jewish population increased from 174,606 to 329,358. In 1931 Jews increased their landholding by 18,585 dunams (4,646 acres), in 1935 by 72,905 dunams: and above all, business and industry enjoyed a 'boom' for which there was no precedent. The Arabs also, although their economy and that of the Jews were to a great extent confined in almost hermetically sealed

[1] *Hazit Haam* (Hebrew newspaper), 16 December 1932.

compartments, derived some warmth from the heat of the 'boom'. One is justified in saying, while conscious that many large groups of Arabs were practically unaffected, that never had the Arabs of Palestine enjoyed such prosperity as in the first years of Sir Arthur Wauchope's régime. But as the Arabs so often say, quoting the writer of Deuteronomy, 'Man does not live by bread alone.' Or to vary the phrase as did some leading Arabs in conversation with a semi-official delegation of English public men, 'Better hunger with liberty and independence, than prosperity and plenty as slaves'. The political desires of the Arabs remained unaffected. On one occasion, in 1933, they manifested themselves in an outbreak which was widespread but not nearly as serious in its immediate effects as those of 1920, 1921 and 1929. This outbreak differed from all its predecessors in that it was not anti-Jewish but anti-Government and anti-British. After the disappointment of 1931 anti-British feeling began to develop and grow among the Arabs. Previously the Zionists or the Jews were the enemies: the war was only with the Government and the British if they got in the way. This time Government was the enemy. Not a Jew was touched. In this respect the outbreak of 1933 was a presage of the far more serious revolt that was to follow. In another respect also the relatively small outbreak of 1933 opened a new chapter. The Arab populations outside began to show an interest in the affairs of Palestine. Events in Palestine had their echoes elsewhere. And unfortunately they were not all merely pro-Arab; some were anti-Jewish. In Transjordan, Syria, Iraq, Egypt and North Africa there were popular movements of sympathy with the Arabs of Palestine, in a few instances accompanied by attacks or attempted attacks on local Jews. Among the Moslems of Jugoslavia and India and even among the Shiites of Persia, between whom and the Sunnites which Moslem sect is prevalent in Palestine, there had for many centuries been hostility, sympathy was also shown.

Although the Jewish half of the Balfour Declaration was being given precedence, the promises to the Arabs or 'the non-Jewish communities in Palestine' were not forgotten. In particular the promise in the Mandate for the 'development of self-governing institutions' was remembered. A legislative council, an early step in this direction, would have been granted in 1922, if the Arabs had not rejected it. The Jews were then quite willing. A few years later, when Lord Plumer was High Commissioner, the promise was repeated, but deferred until the newly elected municipal councils had settled down in their work. Sir John Chancellor in 1929 was satisfied that the time was ripe for a legislative council. The project was then temporarily abandoned, avowedly as a punishment of the Arabs, who had in the meanwhile moved from their intransigent attitude of 1922, for the outbreak. Successive commissions of inquiry had recommended some such measure as desirable and equitable. Secretaries of State from Mr. Winston Churchill through all of his successors had favoured the introduction of such a measure. The only question was one of appropriate occasion. It was in these circumstances that Sir Arthur Wauchope with apparent practical unanimity behind him, hoped to crown his term of office, which had been extended for a second period of five years, by the setting up and successful working of a legislative council. The proposed council followed mainly the lines of the abortive one of 1922. It was a very long distance from any sort of self-government. It was in effect an advisory and consultative council that was contemplated and nothing more. But it was a beginning, a plain beginning to all who saw it. Between 1923 and 1935 the relative proportions of the Arab and Jewish populations had altered, and to the same extent the proportion of Arab and Jewish representatives was to be varied. The new Council was to be in part elected, in part nominated, but differing in this from its predecessor, the official element was to be but a small proportion, five members out of twenty-eight.

Apart from the value of the measure as a step in the fulfilment of the promise to set up self-governing institutions and the consequent assuagement of at least a part of one of the grievances of the Arabs, the proposal had two great advantages. Under the existing system Jew and Arab never met. The Zionist had the right, and held to it very jealously, of being consulted by the Government on all proposed measures that might affect the Jewish population, which were almost all legislative proposals and executive actions. The Arabs without this statutory right were also frequently consulted through their representative body. But except on some not very important departmental committees and municipal councils, the Jewish and Arab leaders or their lieutenants never met one another. Neither knew nor wanted to know the arguments of the other side for or against a proposed course. A legislative council at which Jews and Arabs were present would force each party to listen to the case of the other side, to answer it and possibly in due course to accept that part of it which seemed reasonable. Secondly one of the misfortunes of Palestine, a land in which every inhabitant is a politician, is that there is no organ in which views on public affairs can be expressed and discussed. The newspaper press, extraordinarily extensive for so small a country, consists solely of propaganda sheets. Every newspaper belongs to a party or a party leader and its sole purpose is to put the view of that party. None would ever think of putting, or if it did be permitted to put, the other point of view. As a consequence neither Jew nor Arab—with of course some important exceptions—had an inkling of the case of the other side. The Legislative Council would, as has been said, compel the leaders on each side to listen to the other, and if as a corollary to the formation of the Council, the daily newspapers of Palestine had been compelled by law to publish an officially supplied summary of the debates their readers would at length learn that their opponents had also a case.

It was at the end of December 1935 that the High Commissioner announced the scheme for a legislative council. The Council was to have full powers of discussion and initiation of legislation so long as the validity of the Mandate was not called into question, but the final decision would always rest with the High Commissioner. The question of Women's Suffrage, which the Jews ardently desired and the Arabs opposed, was left to each community to settle for itself. Since the electorates were to be communal, this was quite practicable. The majority of the Arab representatives accepted without much hesitation the proposal, while holding themselves free to require amendments in detail. The Jewish representatives, the successors of those who had accepted Mr. Churchill's similar, but not quite so favourable, scheme, rejected the new one forthwith. They had also moved from their earlier position and no longer wanted any glimmer of self-government until they were assured of a majority. This attitude of the Jews of Palestine was quite unexpected. The Government and the High Commissioner had expected that any opposition that would have been raised would have come from the Arabs. Of the Jews, in view of the past and of the very sympathetic manner in which they had been treated in other directions, the High Commissioner at any rate felt assured. But he was mistaken. A great agitation arose throughout Jewry. The subject was raised in the House of Commons where the lead against a legislative council was taken by Mr. Churchill. The House of Commons showed itself very lukewarm in its support of the Government. The Government might nevertheless have proceeded with its programme, but the debate in the House of Commons being reported and as usual exaggerated in Palestine, reacted on the Arab mentality there. All well-informed observers had for some years expected a new and more serious Arab rising. It came in April 1936, the disappointment over the failure of the Legislative Council proposals and the apparently resolutely unfriendly attitude of the British House of Commons being undoubtedly among the contributory causes, if not the deciding factor.

CHAPTER IX

BRITAIN AND THE MANDATE

British Sympathy with the Jews: A Twofold Obligation: Jewish Friendliness towards Britain: Britain and the Arabs: The Influence of the Extremists: The British, the Scapegoat: Interference by the Amateur: Parliament and the Administration: Balfour on the Mandate: The Mandates Commission.

AS HAS been suggested in an earlier chapter a widespread sympathetic interest with the Jews has prevailed among the English at least since the earlier years of the seventeenth century. In fact it may be said to go back to the Reformation in England, for *Josippon*, the pseudo-Josephus, was in an English translation one of the most popular of books as long ago as 1558. This book purported to be a post-biblical history of the Jews and its popularity could have been based only on the desire of the English for a knowledge of the subsequent history of the people to which the heroes of the Bible belonged, a history connecting these latter and their people with the contemporary Jews. A few decades later the Puritan Movement increased still further this interest in the Jews which remained sympathetic. After the re-settlement of the Jews in England never was any hostility towards them shown except on the part of individuals, for the most part blackmailers, or on the occasion of very infrequent and ephemeral spasms of hysteria such as that which arose around the Naturalization controversy of 1753. Friendly interest in the

Jews has always been rooted deep in the English character and closely allied with this interest has been a desire to show practical sympathy with those of them who suffered abroad. It is unnecessary to give a full record even of the intervention of British Governments with those of the Continent on behalf of their Jews. It is sufficient to mention the representations made by the Government of George II, with success, to the Empress Maria Theresa when she had decided to expel her Jewish subjects from Bohemia, the action of Beaconsfield and Salisbury at the Berlin Congress on behalf of the helot Jews of the newly created Kingdom of Roumania and the attempted influence exercised by British Governments on the Czar of Russia in behalf of the Jewish victims of his persecution. The story of British protection of the Jews of Palestine and other parts of the Ottoman Empire has been narrated, although inadequately, in the foregoing pages. The issue of the Balfour Declaration and the subsequent acceptance of the Mandate for Palestine incorporating its terms were therefore in direct succession to previous actions by British Governments.

The motives of the British Government in issuing the Declaration and in accepting the Mandate were mixed, as motives, political as well as personal, frequently are. This longstanding sympathy was certainly one of them. The British Government, and the British people behind it, genuinely wanted to benefit Jewry and thought that in accepting the Mandate they would be able to do so. But the British Government in benefiting the Jews, in performing the act of generosity and justice, did not wish to commit an injustice against any other people. Hence in the Mandate itself there was a twofold obligation, to favour 'the establishment in Palestine of a National Home for the Jewish people', and at the same time to safeguard 'the civil and religious rights of existing non-Jewish communities'. Successive British Governments believed that by the application of a policy of moderate Zionism, of reasonable Zionism, Jews could be benefited and Arabs, to say the least, not harmed. Successive spokesmen of British Governments have repeatedly emphasized this dual responsibility and the Mandates Commission and Council of the League have recognized it. It appears in the Passfield White Paper where it was again emphasized that the two responsibilities were not incompatible, and was repeated to the League of Nations in the same year. In the Statement of Policy of 8 September 1936, made in the midst of the Arab Rebellion, the affirmation, with the corollary that the two obligations were not irreconcilable, was again repeated. Mr. Churchill, to quote Mr. Lloyd George again, in an address to the Imperial Cabinet in June 1921 and in the presence of Dominion statesmen, stated the British policy clearly. 'To do our best to make an honest effort to give the Jews a chance to make a National Home there for themselves. ... If, in the course of many years, they become a majority in the country, they naturally would take it over. (Mr. Meighen: *Pro rata* with the Arab?) *Pro rata* with the Arab. We made an equal pledge that we would not turn the Arab off his land or invade his political and social rights.'[1] According to Lord Curzon, as reported by Mr. Lloyd George,[2] the words 'civil rights' in the Mandate included 'all ordinary rights', even

[1] *The Truth about the Peace Treaties*, p. 1193.
[2] *idem*, p. 1174.

156   PALESTINE: A POLICY

political rights as interpreted by the French, and the Italian and French statesmen, who were present on the occasion, agreed.

The Zionists on their part have passed many resolutions to the affect that they have no desire or intention to affect unfavourably the welfare of the Arabs and that the fulfilment of their programme would not harm them. Dr. Weizmann, when he appeared before the Peace Conference in 1919, specifically included the safeguarding of 'the established rights of the present non-Jewish population' among the Zionist requirements, and in an interview in 1932, said:

'We are attempting to build a home in Palestine and we are conscious that this building can only be successful if it will be done in co-operation with the peoples and population of Palestine. We are coming into Palestine not as conquerors. We are coming into Palestine not to dominate anybody. We are coming to build up Palestine together with the people there, taking our place according to our merits and our achievements. The other people in Palestine, the Arabs and Christians, have to recognize that we have a right to do what we intend to do. Just as we recognize that Palestine is going to be the common homeland for Jews and Arabs, we want the Arabs to recognize that we have a right to come into Palestine to establish ourselves there, not on the back of anybody, but with them, to work and create new values of which Palestine is capable. . . . Since the War and even before the War there has been a striving on the part of the Arab people for a revival, and being anxious for the revival of the scattered Jewish people, we treat with respect and reverence any attempt at revival amongst other people.'[1]

And again:

'Coming not as conquerors but with peace in our hearts and minds, we who still have a great deal of the East and have gone through Eastern schools, could interpret the West to the East and the East to the West and we could perform an act of civilization which no other people could perform—to serve as a bridge between two cultures that watch each other to-day with suspicion but might be united to-morrow.'[2]

The traditional British friendliness towards the Jews was always fully reciprocated. As has already been indicated there were many occasions on which large foreign Jewish communities had full justification for a feeling of gratitude towards the British. Over the past century or two a pro-British tradition had grown and developed among the Jews in most countries, in those such as Russia, Roumania and the Moslem lands in which the Jewish inhabitants were second or third class citizens, perhaps one should say subjects but not citizens. To the Jews of these lands Britain was not

[1] *Celebrities of our Time*, by Herman Bernstein, pp. 238–9 (An interview).

[2] *ibid*, p. 241. Writing to *The Times* some years earlier in a correspondence that followed the Manifesto of the British non-Zionists after the issue of the Balfour Declaration (see p. 112) he had said: 'The Zionists are not demanding in Palestine monopolies or exclusive privileges, nor are they asking that any part of Palestine should be administered by a Chartered Company to the detriment of others. It always was and remains a cardinal principle of Zionism as a democratic movement that all races and sects in Palestine should enjoy full justice and liberty.'

only a sort of protector, but also the land of liberty, the fortunate inhabitants of which, independent of origin or religion, could live their own lives sharing with their neighbours all the blessings of freedom and in many instances of relative prosperity, no man suffering disability on account of his race or religion but being judged simply on his merits. To the Jew England was the ideal land of the biblical promise where 'they shall sit every man under his vine and under his fig tree'. Until a generation ago England was open to all who wished to enjoy her hospitality. Many took advantage of the opportunity and Britain did not suffer on the whole on account of her generosity. A list of those citizens of foreign parentage or even of foreign birth whose contributions to the intellectual, moral and material wealth of the country and the Empire no one can honestly deny, is evidence of this. But for the last two decades all parts of the British Empire have been in effect closed to Jewish immigrants, apart from, in the latter years, some thousands of the victims of the Nazi Terror. Similarly, and to an even greater extent relatively, the United States has closed its gates in the faces of Jewish immigrants and even refugees. If all these gates were opened, despite the far wider opportunities of North America, the flow of Jewish migration would turn mainly towards the British Empire, attracted by the century-old tradition of British friendliness. Even in Palestine, before the days of Nazism, there was always an appreciably large number of newcomers from Eastern Europe anxious to obtain visas for one part or other of the British Empire who explained, when questioned, that they had come to Palestine believing that it was easier there to secure a visa for

England or Australia or South Africa than in their own homes.

Thus there had long been a moral alliance between Britain and Jewry. But there was also a somewhat similar feeling, dating back at least a century, between the British and the Arabs. The British, of course on a far smaller scale, have had for long a sympathetic interest in the welfare of the Arabs, especially those of Palestine and to a less extent Syria, among whom missionaries and doctors had worked, and who were known by many British travellers. To the Arabs, England was also the land of liberty, and during the long drawn out death struggles of the Ottoman Empire, when every one knew that its end was approaching but no one could say when it would arrive, the Arabs of Palestine and of Syria, excluding perhaps the Lebanon, looked forward hopefully to a British protectorate. The Arabs also knew Britain to be their friend. It was thus that when the dissolution did come Jew and Arab were unanimous in their vote for a British protectorate of Palestine, and, if the wishes of the inhabitants of Syria—Arabs, Druses, Alawites and the few Jews also—had been given consideration, that country also would have come under British protection. The King-Crane Commission, when it went to the Levant to ascertain the wishes of the populations, found a desire for American protection. This was not unnatural since the Commission, although supposed to be sent by the Allied and Associated Powers, was entirely an American one. But as the alternative to an American protection, a British one was always asked, from the Taurus to the Sinai Peninsula.

Thus apart from consideration for abstract justice, British sympathies, intensified by the confidence that

Britain received, made British policy find a basis on consideration for Arab as well as Jewish claims.

But the British did not find their task in Palestine as easy as they had expected. Not that they expected an easy one. They realized that their position there could never be without difficulty. But the difficulties were far greater than they or any one had contemplated. They found themselves as it were between the upper and the nether millstones, between an irresistible force and an immovable body, and this position was by no means pleasant. Jewish and Arab ambitions which might once have been reconciled if there had been moderation and statesmanship on both sides—not on the part of an individual here and there, but on that of those who had charge of the fortunes of both parties—drifted farther and farther apart. The extremists on both sides—on the Arab side more quickly than on the Jewish—gained more and more influence, and the hope of a bi-national state, the ambition of Ahad Ha'Am and of his disciple Dr. Weizmann, seemed to become less and less capable of realization. An Arab State was the ideal of the one side, a Jewish State became to an ever greater extent that of the other. In the one, taking the term in the fullest, clearest sense, there could be no room for Jewish citizens: in the other full Arab citizens would be equally out of the question.[1] And yet neither ideal was attainable. With an Arab majority in the population a Jewish State of this character was inconceivable: with a Jewish population as large as it had already grown an Arab State was equally so. In Palestine all men, and very

---

[1] It is not desired to suggest that either the Arabs or the Jews desired a State of this character, but this is the logical meaning of the terms, as distinguished from that of 'Palestinian State.'

many women also, are politicians, but the level of a statesmanlike outlook is extraordinarily low, according to Western standards. In choosing an object one never takes practicabilities into consideration: it is only one's wishes—and these seldom moderate ones—that count.

Both parties felt themselves balked of their, to them legitimate, end. In their disappointment both looked round for a scapegoat and the obvious one was the Protecting Power and in particular its officers who, in accordance with the traditions of the Civil Service, had no means of defence. Moreover the population fell into two parts, one dynamic, the other static. The ambitions of the Jews seemed to be without limit. The Arabs were equally determined to keep all that they had. Here was the problem of the irresistible force and the immovable body, and the British Government, still more the Palestine Administration, found itself between the two. If the Jews found a hindrance in the path of their hectic rush the Administration had put it there. If the Arabs lost a position in commerce, in land-holding, in office, even in private employment, the Government had helped to oust them. Members of another people would have blown up and given a Roland for an Oliver. Fortunately the British are more phlegmatic, more aloof, perhaps more slow and heavy. They let all the abuse and attacks pass them by and went on with their task of administering the country, to the best of their ability and as far as the available means would allow, in the interest of all of its inhabitants.

If the Palestine administration and the British Government behind them had been left to perform their task, the situation would certainly never have become worse than it ultimately became. More probably it would never have become so bad. The Government of Palestine was and is responsible, however, to Parliament and to some extent to the Council of the League of Nations. Members of the House of Commons are responsible to their constituents and in a number of constituencies Zionists and their friends were very active. And as Sir Ronald Storrs has pointed out no member has Arab constituents. Members of Parliament cannot be expected to be authorities on all the subjects that come before them for consideration and very few had any knowledge, beyond that to be obtained from propaganda literature, of the Palestine problem. A few had been to Palestine and therefore considered themselves *the* authorities on the subject, but a week or two in the country under careful guidance and without any knowledge of Hebrew and above all of Arabic, cannot teach even the ABC of the subject. Thus Parliament consisted and consists of, apart from the members of the Government some of whom are real authorities, supporters who are determined to vote for the Government right or wrong, a small number of other men with first-hand knowledge, the professional opposition not always confined to members of the Opposition parties, members suffering from the pressure of a section of their constituents, and self-constituted authorities and advocates of one side or the other, with a Palestine visa on their passports as their diploma. At the Council of the League of Nations and its Mandates Commission other influences came into effect. Thus the actions of the Palestine Administration, often even in trivial matters of routine, were subject to continuous criticism, and the Government, no matter of what political complexion, always called upon to defend its policy and even its administration.

With the exception of a debate in the House of Lords in June 1922, Parliament has consistently shown itself sympathetic to the Jewish point of view and anxious to do its best for the success of the Zionist experiment. At times it has gone so far on this road as to overlook the Arab point of view entirely, with consequent reactions in disappointment, almost despair, in Palestine. The occasion of the House of Lords debate was the acceptance of the Mandate which the supporters of the resolution argued should be postponed until its terms had been modified so as to provide greater safeguards for Arab rights and interests. Balfour himself took part in the debate in defence of the policy with which his name is connected, this being his first participation in a discussion in the Upper House. He, of course, opposed the motion. He argued that a Jewish government was not necessarily a consequence of the establishment of a Jewish national home. In fact he could conceive of no greater safeguard for the Arab political interests than the institution of the Mandate, for its administration would be jealously watched as under a magnifying glass. The suggestion that the terms of the Mandate or the British Administration since the occupation of Palestine had been unjust to the Arab population was to him ridiculous. The House, however, did not share Lord Balfour's views and the condemnatory motion was carried by a majority of two to one. A fortnight later the House of Commons took the contrary view. The subject was also raised by Conservative critics. Mr. Winston Churchill, then Colonial Secretary, defended the Government policy as fulfilling the promise

164   PALESTINE: A POLICY

of the Balfour Declaration without injustice to the Arabs. The House was behind him and the Government obtained an overwhelming majority.

These debates were in the days of optimism when the practical application of the Mandate lay still in the future. Although there had been some warnings that the road ahead was not consistently smooth, the hitherto indefinite constitutional position was held responsible for most of the difficulties that had arisen. Once the Mandate was adopted and the constitutional position perfectly clear these difficulties would disappear. So it was widely believed, or at any rate hoped. The foregoing narrative will show that these hopes were not realized. Instead of diminishing, the number of difficulties increased and at the same time became more complex. Palestine also entered into British politics. It became a stick with which to beat the sitting Government. It has never become entirely a party question on which all the members of the Government party vote in support and all those on the other side against. There have always been some dissidents on both sides. But to a very large extent the Opposition has found it its duty to oppose the Government policy, whichever party might be in power, and similarly the members of the party in power have approved that policy, whatever it might be and no matter how quickly and completely it might change. The greatest anomalies were ex-secretaries of state arguing fiercely against the policy which they had forwarded when in office, and prominent members of Government taking refuge in silence when asked to reconcile the policy of 1940 with their intense opposition to the less objectionable one, from the Zionist point of view, of 1930.

One of the most important debates on Palestine was held in the House of Commons on 17 November 1930, after the issue of the Passfield White Paper which had caused such consternation in Jewish circles. The attack was led by Mr. Lloyd George, who had been Prime Minister when the Balfour Declaration was issued. Rather extravagantly he denounced the policy that had been announced, which was after all only an elaboration of that for which his own Government had been responsible in 1922, not only as contrary to the spirit of the Balfour Declaration but as in effect a revocation of the Mandate. He was supported by a number of Conservative speakers, to whom members of the Government, at a later date to be among the strongest supporters of Zionist claims, replied. Possibly this debate contributed towards the issue not long afterwards of the Macdonald Letter which was intended to mollify the Zionists and as it pleased them, to the same extent disappointed and enraged the Arabs. In 1936 there were further debates in Parliament. The proposed Legislative Council was on this occasion the immediate topic of discussion. It suffered severe criticism, for different reasons, in both Houses, In fact the objections raised would probably have led to the abandonment of the proposals, if the outbreak to which these parliamentary discussions—less than friendly to so large an extent to the Arab cause—were unquestionably a contribution, had not supervened. With Palestine in revolt, and the whole of the constitutional position on the edge of the melting-pot, the question of a legislative council and its powers was for the moment no longer of practical consequence.

The Mandates Commission of the League of Nations

also was not always helpful to the Mandatory Power in its very difficult task, but there was never reason to complain of factious criticism on its part. The Council of the League was far less critical and as a rule approved without question whatever line the Mandatory Power found it necessary to take. The terms of the Mandate, with its interpretation as explained in the Churchill White Paper, were unanimously accepted by the Council of the League. In 1924, when Palestine was suffering from a minor economic depression, the Mandates Commission in its first report on the administration of the country suggested that there had been a departure from the lines laid down in the Churchill White Paper inasmuch as immigration in the previous years seemed to have passed the limits of economic absorptive capacity. It also emphasized the twofold obligation, to Arabs as well as Jews. The gross immigration figures in the year under review were 7991!

The following year, however, the Commission was less critical. At the meeting of June 1930, held after the outbreak of 1929 with the Report of the Shaw Commission before it, it was far more severe. It criticized in particular the Mandatory's administration. The Mandates Commission charged the British Government with failing to assure that security of person and property which was 'the essential condition for development of the Jewish National Home,' and also with paying insufficient attention to 'the social and economic adaptation of the Arab population to the new conditions due to Jewish immigration,' whereby the Arabs had been unfavourably affected. Moreover the Mandatory Power might, in its opinion, have done more to bring about that economic 'fusion of interests which is the best possible means of developing a sense of solidarity and blunting the edge of antagonism'. As for the competing memoranda and petitions of the Zionists and the Arabs, it accepted the case of neither of the litigants. It did, however, accept the view expressed by the British Government 'that the obligations laid down by the Mandate in regard to the two sections of the population are of equal weight' and expressed the further opinion that there was no necessary priority for the establishment of a National home over the development of self-governing institutions. The British Government did not take the criticisms of the Mandates Commission in very good part and replied somewhat sharply, but the controversy was eased by the diplomacy of the Council of the League which referred the Mandates Commission Report to the British Government with a request that it should 'adopt such measures as it thinks fit to give effect to the recommendations and conclusions'. Unfortunately the Mandates Commission feels itself precluded from visiting Palestine and studying its problems on the spot. There are arguments against such visits, but on balance they would probably be advantageous.

CHAPTER X

THE PEEL COMMISSION

The 1936 Rebellion: Sympathy of Foreign Arabs: A Royal Commission: The Mandate Unworkable: Partition of Palestine: Parliament: The League of Nations: Arab Opinion: The Zionist Attitude: The Technical Commission: End of Partition: An Abortive Conference: A New Government Policy.

THE LONG expected outbreak occurred on 19 April 1936 and as was almost equally expected, arose out of some trivial incident exaggerated by rumour. Similar incidents had occurred a hundred times before and exaggeration and rumour are always rife in Palestine. However, apparently on the previous occasions the moment had not arrived: on this occasion it had. The outbreak opened as on previous occasions with attacks, in Jaffa, on inoffensive Jewish passers-by, but it very quickly developed first into a widespread attack on the Jews and soon into an open rebellion against the Government. This rebellion was active and also passive. The latter development even preceded the former, for within a few days of the first murder, representative committees that sprang into existence in all the Arab centres proclaimed a general strike until the national demands of the Arabs were granted[1], and were sufficiently

[1] These were (a) The establishment of democratic government, (b) Prohibition of the transfer of land to Jews and the securing of the small cultivator in his holding, (c) The suspension of Jewish immigration until new principles based on the real economic absorptive capacity of the country had been adopted, and (d) The immediate stoppage of illegal immigration.

THE PEEL COMMISSION

insistent and strong to force or induce the central committee in Jerusalem, the Arab Higher Committee, in which all the several Arab parties had sunk their differences, to adopt this policy. The rebellion varied at times in intensity but lasted over three years and then was put down only by the exercise of considerable military power. The strike lasted six months, supported by all sections of the population despite their sufferings. It was of course not universal, but it was sufficiently widespread to make it unique. Superficially it was a failure, for the objects for which it was proclaimed were not attained, but in illustrating the determination and unity of the Arabs of Palestine it was successful and formed a material element in forcing the authorities to give consideration to the Arab case.

The outbreak was inevitable and would have come in any circumstances unless perhaps there had been a complete reversal of British policy. The main cause was the disappointment and apparent hopelessness of the Arab position, coupled with an ever increasing fear for the future. These alone might not have led to an outbreak at that time. But there were the examples of their neighbours and kinsmen, Egypt, Iraq and Syria, before them. These countries had also demanded self-government and had been refused. The reply in all three cases had been a revolt and the demands had been granted. In Syria the grant was not yet effective, but a definite promise of self-government and independence on the Iraquian and Egyptian model by an early date had been given. In Syria also the last step taken by the people was a general strike which after seven weeks forced the French to capitulate.

Another feature of the outbreak was the widespread

and, as time passed, increasing sympathy on the part of the Arabs and Moslems of other countries with their kinsmen and co-religionists in Palestine in the struggle. Even as long ago as 1929 one of the difficulties with which the Government of Palestine had to cope in putting down the disturbance was the sympathy, which reached the verge of bursting into activity, of the Bedouin of Transjordan with the Palestine Arabs, encouraged by the extravagant rumours that were current among them. In 1936 and as time passed a similar and even more threatening movement arose among them and it taxed all the resources of the Amir of Transjordan and of the British Resident, Sir Henry Cox, to keep them within their own boundaries. A similar movement arose among the Bedouin of Iraq who were also restrained with difficulty, and a popular movement of sympathy spread, as time passed, as far west as Morocco and east as India. This pro-Arab movement, which was at the same time anti-Jewish, was unquestionably to some extent fomented from centres that were bitterly anti-Jewish and as subsequent events showed equally anti-British and therefore anxious to cause Britain trouble everywhere and in all circumstances. Moreover the Arabs of Palestine appealed to their kinsmen everywhere for assistance. Their appeal was probably more effective than the propaganda of powers whom none of the peoples to whom it was directed had any reason to trust or to thank. In fact it was so effective that the Governments of the Arab States were forced to intervene and offer their services to bring the rebellion to an end. In the end they did so but not without difficulty, for the British Government would offer no terms but demanded a surrender. The prestige of Iraq, Egypt and the other

THE PEEL COMMISSION

States was, however, high in Palestine and although the Arab Higher Committee could obtain no promises it trusted to the influence of its friends to secure for it in the end the terms to which it considered itself morally and also legally entitled. The Peel Commission was much impressed by this intervention by the Arab States. 'If we were to pick out the feature of the late "disturbances" which on a general view seems to us the most striking and far-reaching, it would be the manner in which they roused the feeling of the Arab world at large against Zionism and its defenders.' In India the Moslems, who are not Arabs, celebrated a 'Palestine Day', held a Pan-India Congress for Palestine, sent a deputation representative not only of the Moslems of India but also of the Moslem rulers to the Viceroy and petitioned the Council of the League of Nations to cancel the Mandate for Palestine altogether.

The British Government very quickly decided that a new investigation of the causes of these outbreaks and of the Arab dissatisfaction was called for and three weeks after the beginning of the outbreak the High Commissioner promised an investigation by a Royal Commission once the strike was called off. But the situation was already out of the hands of the Arab Higher Committee if it had ever been in their control, and in order to keep any control of events the leaders had by now to keep very close behind their followers. These followers were determined to continue the strike until their demands were granted; so the offer of a Royal Commission had to remain in suspense. The condition was later varied so as to take the form of an end of the disturbances, but even this had to be abandoned in the end, and when the Royal Commission, under the

Chairmanship of Viscount Peel, arrived in Palestine in November the country was not at peace although the intensity of the outbreak was much modified. A further eight months elapsed before the Commission presented its report. These months were marked by continuous unrest and disturbance but not of such intensity as that of the first few months of the outbreak.

The Report of the Royal Commission was hailed as an epoch-making document. It certainly was most impressive in size, in diction, and in its attention to detail. When, however, people began to read it, to examine it, to consider critically its conclusions and recommendations, opinion began to be revised. One fact stood out clearly; the revolutionary recommendation which the Commissioners made did not issue from the facts that they had marshalled with so much diligence and care or from the arguments they deduced from them. The conclusion seemed to be an afterthought, to have been conceived after the greater part of the Report had been written. The first instruction in the warrant appointing the commission was to ascertain the underlying causes of the disturbances. The reply to this was clear. The Commissioners agreed with all their predecessors in former commissions and committees of inquiry, that the causes of these recurrent outbreaks were 'the desire of the Arabs for National independence and their hatred and fear of the Jewish National Home.' On this occasion the causes had been aggravated, they found, by the success of Arabs elsewhere in gaining their independence, by the greatly increased Jewish immigration in recent years, largely an immigration of refugees from persecution in Central Europe, by the advantages Jews had over Arabs in putting their case before the British

THE PEEL COMMISSION

public, Government and Parliament, by the increased purchase of land in Palestine by Jews, by the militant nationalism of a considerable part of the new Jewish population and by general uncertainty as to what the Government's permanent policy really was. In short the causes of the outbreak were the terms of the Mandate and the manner in which they had been put into effect.

The second instruction in the Warrant was to inquire into the manner in which the Mandate was being administered. Here the Commission had great opportunities, for the Zionists showered on it complaints against the Administration, complaints of principle and complaints of detail. The Commission was fortunately spared a similar list of complaints by the Arabs which they would have been well prepared to make if they had not boycotted the Commission until its last week in the country. The Commission investigated these numerous complaints or at any rate the more serious of them and came to the conclusion that with one exception they had no basis. The exception was the charge that the Government of Palestine had not afforded that protection of the law-abiding Jewish population, to which they were entitled. To this the Commission agreed. It moreover made a number of recommendations regarding administration, some of which pleased the Zionists and some did not. The Commissioners were, however, compelled to point out that the adoption of these recommendations would not '"remove" the grievances nor "prevent their recurrences"'. They were merely palliatives. The sympathy of the Commissioners with the Palestine Administration and its members was undisguised. 'We doubt whether there is any country in the world where the position of the Government is less enviable

174   PALESTINE: A POLICY

than that of the Government of Palestine.'[1] Quoting a Jewish witness: 'We are not an easy people to deal with. First of all to a Jew who comes from the East of Europe, an official is a "*Tchinovnik*". He must be corrupt. He must be hostile. He is the enemy of the public. It takes many years to drum into their heads that the British official is, to begin with, the servant of the public, a friend. . . . There was a constant tug of war and the Government was accused by both sides of either being pro-Arab or pro-Jew, and it has developed into the feeling that if one is pro-Arab one must necessarily be anti-Jew or *vice versa*, which is not necessary at all'. An honest Arab witness might have said the same, substituting 'Arab' for 'Jew'. The comment of the Commission is 'No one could tour in Palestine without realizing the extremely difficult position of the British official, and, indeed, of the whole Administration.'[2]

After the Commission had inquired into the manner in which the Mandate had been and was being implemented, it was instructed to consider the grievances put forward by the Arabs and the Jews and if it found that there were any legitimate grievances to recommend measures for remedying them. As has already been suggested the main Arab grievance was the existence of the Mandate, that of the Zionist that the Government was not taking sufficient steps to render possible the creation of a Jewish State in the near future. Obviously no recommendation or series of recommendations could satisfy both parties and no recommendation that touched on principle could fail to enrage one side or the

[1] Report p. 136.
[2] Page 163.

THE PEEL COMMISSION

other. The Commissioners, quickly recognizing this and accepting a dual obligation under the terms of the Mandate to Arabs as well as Jews, came to the conclusion that the Mandate was unworkable and that it was useless to attempt to make it work. To prepare for the event of the Government not sharing their views they put forward a series of recommendations, palliatives as they described them, for the most part tending to reduce the rights and privileges the Jews already had in Palestine. But the Commission had no faith in these palliatives and did not conceal their lack of faith. Their choice was a revolutionary alternative which carried with it the cancellation of the Mandate.

In arriving at this conclusion the Commission adopted the view that the obligations to Jews and Arabs laid down in the Mandate were irreconcilable and that the Mandate was therefore unworkable. It was impossible they concluded to fulfil obligations to both parties in any one territory. 'As our inquiry proceeded, we became more and more persuaded that, if the existing Mandate continued, there was little hope of lasting peace in Palestine, and at the end we were convinced that there was none.'[1] They therefore recommended that Palestine, a country as small as Wales and with wealth and natural resources only a fraction of those of Wales, should be divided into three parts. One should form a Jewish sovereign independent State: a second a similar Arab State; the third that would include the Holy Places should remain with no special obligations to Jews, in effect a British Crown Colony. In their respective states the Jews and the Arabs could do as they wished, but as the Arab State, which could contain little

[1] Page 380.

cultivable land and no port, was doomed to insolvency from its initiation, the Government of the Jewish State should pay it an annual subvention. The principal racial minorities, which, according to the frontiers provisionally drawn in the Report, would have amounted to 225,000 Arabs out of a total population of about 475,000 in the Jewish State, should be provided for to a large extent by exchange, voluntary if this were possible, otherwise compulsory. As however the number of Jews to be left under Arab rule would have been only about 1,250, exchange was obviously impracticable. In foreign affairs and security against attack the precedents of Egypt and Iraq should be followed.

The Commission themselves had little faith in this solution. The very faint praise with which they damned it showed this. 'The practical difficulties (of Partition) seemed too great. And great they unquestionably are. The closer the question is examined, the clearer they stand out. We do not underestimate them. They cannot be brushed aside. Nevertheless, when one faces up to them, those difficulties do not seem so insuperable as the difficulties inherent in the continuance of the Mandate or in any other alternative arrangement which has been proposed to us or which we ourselves could devise. *Partition seems to offer at least a chance of ultimate peace. We can see none in any other plan.*'[1]

There had been rumours for some weeks before the issue of the Report of the conclusions it would reach and the suggestion of a partition of the country had caused consternation in many quarters, Jews, Zionists and non-Zionists, were practically unanimous in their objections, and Zionist organizations met in all lands

[1] Page 376. The italics are mine.

THE PEEL COMMISSION

to register in advance their objection to the threatened course. As early as 26 April, the World Zionist Executive, sitting in Jerusalem, formally resolved that the Zionist Organisation would resist any attempt to curtail the rights of the Jews, as defined in the Mandate, either by partition or any other measure. To this unanimity there was, however, one very important exception. Dr. Weizmann, who after all was the one man who counted in Zionism, at any rate the only man whose views were considered by the British Government, refused to commit himself. He declined, as he said, to deal with a hypothetical situation. The impression spread and gained force that he differed from the other exponents of Zionist opinion and was sympathetic to the anticipated conclusion of the Royal Commission. The Government or the Colonial Secretary almost certainly held this view. The latter, Mr. Ormsby-Gore, later Lord Harlech, had given a good part of the previous twenty years to the furtherance of the Zionist ideal in which he was a sincere believer. The failure of this ideal to be translated into reality undoubtedly caused him deep disappointment. While the Commission was still sitting and earlier, he and his colleagues had been urged from all quarters this time to come to a decision and to stand by it, not once again to repeat the indecisions and uncertainties with which the whole course of Palestinian history had been bedevilled during the previous twenty years. He knew that Dr. Weizmann was not opposed to the principle of Partition and believed, as he had reason to believe, that he was the greater part of the Zionist Movement. Simultaneously with the Report of the Royal Commission was therefore published a Government White Paper announcing the acceptance of its main recommendation, and that the Government intended to put it into force.

The Government had accepted the policy of Partition wholeheartedly, but there was no such unanimity elsewhere. Parliament on the whole accepted the lead of the Government but with much unconcealed misgiving and hesitation. Informed criticism was summed up by Lord Samuel who, as a former High Commissioner of Palestine, was one of the best informed members of Parliament. 'The Commission seem to have gone to the Versailles Treaty and picked out all the most difficult and awkward provisions it contained. They have put a Saar, a Polish Corridor and half a dozen Danzigs and Memels into a country the size of Wales.' The House of Commons refused to accept the policy at once. It authorized the Government to put the proposal before the League of Nations with a view to enabling it, after adequate inquiry, to present to Parliament a definite scheme which should take into account all the recommendations of the Report. The Permanent Mandates Commission of the League examined the Report and the representatives of the British Government at great length in July and August 1937. It also was not enamoured of Partition. In fact it agreed with the Government only in the view that the present system could not continue. Recognizing, however, that the responsibility for the government of the country rested not with itself but with the British, it refrained from making any positive suggestions. It thought that further consideration should be given and that at any rate the creation of two independent States should be postponed. The most to which it could look forward for the immediate future was a sort of cantonization,

THE PEEL COMMISSION

that is to say a wide system of local self-government in the district predominantly Jewish, and in another predominantly Arab, both to remain for the present at any rate under British Mandate, ultimately perhaps to be separated. It agreed that the present Mandate having been proved by both the Royal Commission and the Mandatory Power, to be unworkable, had thereby become so or almost so, if it had not previously completely failed. In the end the Council of the League granted the request of the British Government and authorized it to explore further the practicability of Partition, but not to put it into effect without referring again to the Council.

Arab opinion, in Palestine and outside, was unanimously opposed to any suggestion of Partition. It opposed it both in principle and in detail. In Palestine an immediate consequence of the Report of the Royal Commission was a recrudescence of the Rebellion which had practically died away while the Commission was hearing evidence and considering its Report. So long as the Commission was sitting there was hope that it would accept the Arab case and that the Government would grant the Arab demands. The Report of the Commission and the Government policy were however a denial of these demands and there seemed nothing but a return to the earlier procedure. While the Arabs of Palestine broke out again in rebellion, the Governments of the neighbouring States took up their cause at Geneva and in Downing Street. In this the lead was taken by the Government of Iraq which spoke in very emphatic terms. Iraq was, however, well supported by the Governments of Egypt, Saudi-Arabia, the Yemen and even Iran. Abdullah, Amir of Transjordan, a dependant of the British Government, was at first inclined to approve of the British policy—it included a considerable extension of his Amirate by the addition to it of the Arab part of Palestine—but when he found his people opposed to it practically to a man, he at once came into line with them. There were popular protests against Partition in Syria, Egypt, Iraq, Tunis, Arabia, India, even a one-day strike in Mecca and Medina, a remarkable illustration of the march of Western ideas. Simultaneously an Arab National Congress, with influential representations from all the Arab countries, was held at Bludan in Syria and resolved that the Arab nation and the Moslem people would continue the struggle for the Arab cause in Palestine. Still more significant was the condemnation by the All-India Moslem League of the policy of Partition, of similar resolutions adopted by a special Palestine Conference convened by it in Calcutta and the setting up by it of a committee for the defence of Palestine.

While the Mandates Commission of the League of Nations was considering the Report of the Royal Commission in Geneva, a Zionist Congress was being held in the neighbouring Zurich. Dr. Weizmann fought hard to get the Congress to approve the policy of Partition, but, despite his great influence and prestige, was not only unable to secure unanimity but even to get a full acceptance of the proposal. Even he admitted that the details of the Royal Commission's scheme, especially the proposed boundaries of the Jewish State, were unacceptable. In this there was no Jew who differed from him. But the most that Dr. Weizmann could get the Zionist Congress to give him was authority to enter into negotiations with the British Government 'with a view to ascertaining the precise terms of His Majesty's Government for the

THE PEEL COMMISSION

proposed establishment of a Jewish State' but with no authority to come to a decision. This resolution was carried by 300 votes to 158, but some 75 members of the majority subsequently announced that their vote must not be taken as acceptance of Partition. The Council of the Jewish Agency which met immediately after the Zionist Congress was even more reserved. After much discussion and grave difference of opinion, in order to preserve unity, it adopted a resolution identical with that of the Zionist Congress, but added a clause to the effect that before Partition was considered the Government should be asked to convene a conference of Jews and Arabs with a view to 'exploring the possibilities of a peaceful settlement between Jews and Arabs in and for an undivided Palestine.' The greater part of the value of this approach was unfortunately taken away by the last few words of the resolution: 'On the basis of the Balfour Declaration and the Mandate'. It must have been obvious that the Arabs would never be willing to enter on discussions on such a prearranged basis. The Zionists might equally have been expected to accept in advance the basis of an Arab State. On the Jewish Agency Council there were not only opponents of the Partition of Palestine, but also of a Jewish State anywhere.

The British Government was by now free to go ahead with its explorations of the practicability of Partition, but it was now delayed by the rebellion which had again broken out. However a technical commission went to Palestine early in 1938, but by now the Government's enthusiasm for its policy had begun to cool and it was clearly hinted to the new commission, in its terms of reference, that it might come to the conclusion that Partition was impracticable. One sub-section in the terms of reference caused much dismay among the Zionists. The most determined of those in favour of Partition had always contended that the boundaries suggested by the Royal Commission were too narrow and must be enlarged. Some went so far as to accept Partition in principle but to demand that nine-tenths of the present territory of Palestine should be included in the new State. None was willing to accept the limits provisionally laid down. In fact it was impossible for them to do otherwise, for the Royal Commission boundaries meant a Zionism without Zion, by the exclusion of Jerusalem, and also a Land of Israel confined for the most part to ancient Philistia with both Samaria and Judaea outside. The terms of reference however suggested not an extension, but a contraction of the boundaries, so as to 'necessitate the inclusion of the fewest possible Arabs and Arab enterprises in the Jewish area and vice versa'. Since the tentative State would have included almost as many Arabs as Jews and since only a few hundred Jews were to have been left to the Arab State, this could only mean a reduction in the extent of the proposed Jewish territory. The Technical Commission read it as such and while reporting in effect that it was impossible to divide Palestine into separate Arab and Jewish States which could have any chance of survival, continued that if nevertheless Partition was determined on the Jewish State would have to be reduced to the size of a small English county, and even that in two detached parts. Partition was already very sick, perhaps hopelessly so. This Report gave it its *coup de grace*. It no longer had a single friend, apart perhaps from its authors.

The British Government had to start afresh. In the

THE PEEL COMMISSION

document in which they announced the abandonment of Partition they also announced their intention to make one more attempt to bring Jews and Arabs together so that they might in co-operation evolve an acceptable constitution for Palestine. They recognized that just as the Jews outside of as well as inside Palestine were deeply interested so were the Arabs of both Palestine and other lands. It was therefore intended to invite representatives of the Arab States to the proposed conference. The Government hoped sincerely for an agreement but warned both parties that if an early agreement did not come about, it would draw up and impose its own policy. The Arab and Jewish representatives duly arrived in London early in 1939, but the two sides never met. There were conferences between the Arab and Government representatives and between the Jewish and Government representatives. There were informal meetings at which representatives of the Arab States and Jewish representatives—the Jewish representation was also very wide, and was by no means confined to Zionists or even non-Zionist members of the Jewish Agency—met, sometimes alone, sometimes in the presence of Government representatives, but the Arabs resolutely refused to meet representatives of the Jewish Agency and thereby, as they feared, give recognition to it and to the Mandate. Mr. Malcolm Macdonald, who had by now become Secretary for the Colonies, worked devotedly and without stint in order to secure if only an approach to an agreement. He himself put forward proposals for a basis of discussion, but the only result of this was the withdrawal of the Jewish representatives altogether. Throughout the proceedings they showed remarkable unanimity despite the different points of view they had previously held. The

PALESTINE: A POLICY

Government suggestions fell far short of the Zionist minimum and therefore had to be rejected out of hand. The Arabs on their part were also dissatisfied with the suggestions, but they were more amenable. They did not break off the discussions, and, after they had left England, these were continued in Cairo. In the end the Government suggestions were somewhat amended and published as the policy the Government intended to put into effect in view of the failure of the Arabs and Jews to come to an agreement.

The new statement of policy[1] opened with a recital of the three main obligations imposed by the Mandate— (1) To place the country under such political, administrative and economic conditions as will secure the establishment in Palestine of a national home for the Jewish people, to facilitate Jewish immigration under suitable conditions, and to encourage, in co-operation with the Jewish Agency, close settlement by Jews on the land. (2) To safeguard the civil and religious rights of all the inhabitants of Palestine irrespective of race and religion, and, whilst facilitating Jewish immigration and settlement, to ensure that the rights and position of other sections of the population are not prejudiced. (3) To place the country under such political, administrative and economic conditions as will secure the development of self-governing institutions. It then went on to say that although an ultimate Jewish State was not precluded by the terms of the Declaration on which the Mandate was based, it was never intended that 'Palestine should be converted into a Jewish State against the will of the Arab population of the country'. In this respect the British Government still abode by the terms of the Churchill

[1] Cmd. 6019 of 1939.

THE PEEL COMMISSION

White Paper.[1] Finally the new statement laid down the Government's intentions for the future. These were in short the establishment within ten years of an independent Palestine State, one in which Jews and Arabs would share in the government and the essential interests of each community would be safeguarded. In the meanwhile the British Government would retain responsibility but the people of Palestine would be given an increasing part in the government of the country. As a first step Palestinians would be put in charge of some of the departments of government, with British advisers and subject to the control of the High Commissioner, and also be appointed to the Executive Council. Ultimately these heads of departments would become ministers. For the moment no steps would be taken in the direction of an elected assembly, but this was a goal that the Government would keep in view. At the end of five years representatives of the people of Palestine would consult with British representatives with a view to the elaboration of a constitution. Provision would be made in this constitution for the safeguarding of the Holy Places and the protection of religious bodies, for the protection of the different communities and for the special position of the Jewish National Home, for the strategic needs of the country and for the safeguarding of the interests of certain foreign countries. If at the end of ten years the creation of an independent state seemed for any reason premature, Britain would consult with representatives of Palestine, the Council of the League of Nations and the neighbouring Governments on the steps to be taken.

In the meanwhile Jewish immigration during the period

[1] See p. 131.

of five years should not exceed the economic absorptive capacity, but also should not exceed ten thousand per annum apart from a further number of 25,000 Jewish refugees to be admitted during the same period. This would raise the Jewish population of Palestine at the end of the period to approximately one third. At the end of that period there should be no further immigration of Jews without the agreement of the Arab population. With regard to land the unanimous recommendations of the several commissions that had inquired into the subject would be adopted and the purchase of further land by Jews limited. The country would for this purpose be divided into three zones. In the one the transfer of land to Jews would be prohibited: in the second such transfer would be permitted only exceptionally: in the third transfer would be free.

The new immigration procedure was put into force at once and when there was an attempt to counter it by the introduction of large parties of unauthorized immigrants, the number of these, as far as they were known or could be estimated, were counted against the quota of authorized immigrants. From the first months of the Civil Administration legislative attempts to safeguard the small agriculturalist dependent for his living on the land had been made but had had too many loopholes to permit its object as a rule to be attained. As time passed this legislation had been amended and strengthened. By the legislation of 1934 the position of a tenant cultivator had been fairly secured and when the rebellion broke out legislation which was intended to benefit similarly small owner-cultivators was in draft. The events of 1936 and the subsequent years, however, pushed this matter aside. This was unfortunate, for although not granting the political demands of the Arabs with regard to land legislation these measures would have gone far to safeguard the position of the very large number of small cultivators, owners or tenants, which in many instances was beginning to be threatened. So far as was publicly known the Government took no further steps for almost a year after the issue of the Statement of Policy of May 1939. International developments in the meanwhile were sufficient to justify almost any delay. In fact, however, the subject was not being neglected and in February 1940 Regulations for the Transfer of Land in Palestine were somewhat unexpectedly issued. These in principle followed the advice of successive commissions and commissioners including the Peel Commission and divided Palestine into three zones as foreshadowed in the Government Statement of Policy. In one other respect the situation moved towards stability. The disturbed conditions of the previous four years had led to hundreds of Arab exiles from Palestine and a large if smaller number of prisoners in Palestine. These fell into several classes. There was the small number of Arab leaders who had been exiled by the Government and in a few instances interned in the Seychelles. There was the very much larger number of Arab refugees in neighbouring lands, afraid to return to Palestine, against some of whom there were definite charges of criminal offences. Those Arabs and Jews imprisoned or interned in Palestine fell into two classes: those who had been convicted of crimes and those who were only under suspicion, against whom presumably convictions could not be obtained. The Government policy with regard to these several classes, put into force by degrees but without delay, was to re-admit to Palestine or release from internment camp, all, with a few important exceptions, who had not been convicted of crime or against whom there was not a sufficient case to justify a prosecution. Those however who had fled from prosecution ran the risk of arrest on their return. The Government did not intend to tolerate crime whoever the perpetrator might be nor did it accept politics as a valid defence.

Both the Arabs and the Jews received the new Government policy with hostility, but there was a great difference in degree between the two. The Jews denounced it as a complete betrayal, as a reversal of all the promises and pledges that had been made to them. They vowed to fight the new policy until it was withdrawn. The Arab hostility was more formal. It was inevitable, since the very letter of their demands had not been granted. They realized, however, that the Government was giving them much and was promising more and there was no real opposition to it. What opposition there was was based on the suspicion that the Government was not altogether acting in good faith and that as on past occasions, so they said, promises that were being made would not be kept.

CHAPTER XI

THE NEXT STEP

The Satisfaction of Competing Rights: Justice to Jew and Arab not Incompatible: Communal Autonomy: A Jewish National Home: Safeguards: A Federation: An Artificial Boundary: A Larger Customs Union, a Necessity: Immigration and Land: A New Arab-Jewish Co-operation.

THE WHITE PAPER of May 1939 was intended to be a step towards the solution of the Palestine Problem, but not a step that went the whole way. It suggested the lines of a solution, lines that the Government was resolved to follow, but it left many details, for instance the all-important ones of the terms of a constitution and of safeguards, to be filled in later. These were deliberately left over until a time when it is hoped that the mutual suspicions and the fear and hatred generated by them will have subsided and it will be possible for Palestinian patriots, Arab and Jewish, to meet and work out together a constitution for their common country. The Problem of Palestine has been said to be that of the irresistible force coming in contact with the immovable body, but it is not that. If it were the problem would be indeed insoluble and statesmen and wellwishers might well despair. It is more the resolution of a conflict between two rights, a very difficult problem, but yet not an insoluble one. Quoting that excellent summary of the problem published by the Royal Institute of International Affairs, 'Great Britain and Palestine, 1915–1939': 'It is the psychological problem of how to reconcile two powerful movements—the time-old yearning of the Jews to return to the Promised Land and to possess a home which is theirs as of right, and the Palestinian Arab desire for promotion to national status.' Looking at the problem from another point of view one might say that it is how to satisfy simultaneously the fully justified and natural longings, determination, of two peoples, as individuals and as communities, for the freedom and liberty that are the birthright of all human beings, freedom not only to live but to develop along their own lines.

The freedom of one individual or of one community to live and develop does not carry with it the refusal to another individual or community to do likewise. There is still room in the world for all of its inhabitants and for many more and there is also room for all the existing communities to develop without injury to others. Even in individual States there is room for different communities to live side by side without detriment to one another, all equal citizens of the state as a whole and at the same time members of their own community. These communities or nationalities exist to-day in many states and have done so for centuries. To-day, with the world as it were in the melting-pot, with aggressive nationalism rampant almost everywhere, and many rulers inspired only by the desire to seize other peoples' lands and oppress and exploit their inhabitants, seems hardly the moment for the toleration of and co-operation with other communities that are different from one's own. But it must always be remembered that the present phase is

THE NEXT STEP

ephemeral and will pass and that for every year that the present state of intolerance reigns there has been a century during which communities and nationalities lived together in friendship. If humanity is to survive, this earlier condition must return and in Palestine it should be easier than elsewhere for humanity to begin to retrace its footsteps. .

The Arabs of Palestine want to secure themselves against being dominated by any other people. They want to be free to live their own lives without interference from any other quarter and with no desire to harm other people, provided that the attainment of their object is possible without doing so. The Jews, so far as they are Zionists, that is to say anxious for the creation of a Jewish National Home in Palestine, have a similar aim. They also wish to secure the freedom and happiness of the Jews as individuals in Palestine and opportunity as a community or nationality to work out and develop their own civilization, their own culture, their own manner of life, without infringing on the liberties of others or the freedom of other communities in the land to follow their example. There are, of course, extremists on both sides, men of aggression who cannot be satisfied if any one else is happy. Neither Jews nor Arabs can be exceptions to the rule of humanity. Most people in Palestine as elsewhere are after all intellectually lazy or impotent and willing to follow their leaders and to do generally as is suggested to them. But in Palestine the deliberate extremists are few and the overwhelming majority of the population would quickly settle down to good relations with their neighbours if they were permitted, not discouraged from doing so, provided that conditions of life were tolerable, that as human beings, and also as Arabs and Jews, at least the minimum to which man is entitled to look forward were attained or within sight.

The Jews want to create in Palestine their National Home. Putting aside for the moment the necessity of defining this term, it can be accepted at once that a National Home, whatever it may be, cannot exist without a Jewish population, of appreciable size and qualitatively self-supporting, healthy in body and mind. The Jews therefore need something more than freedom as individuals and as a community. They need what the Arabs have had for centuries, a population to enjoy these benefits. There is another factor in the Jewish side of the problem. The present period is unfortunately one of intense Jewish suffering. The cries of despair and of agony from Central and Eastern Europe strike against the ears of numberless kinsmen and devoted friends who are living in Palestine and in other lands of relative happiness. Apart from the call of the blood there is also that feeling of sympathy with suffering and the desire to alleviate it that is so deeply rooted and prevalent in the general Jewish character. Palestine has consequently taken on the role not only of the Jewish National Home but also of a land of refuge, almost at the moment the only land of refuge to which the friends and kinsmen of individual Jews and suffering Jewry as a whole can escape. This new role unfortunately has not only increased the difficulties of the problem but has jeopardized the ideal of the Zionists, dependent on a careful selection of immigrants, the creation in Palestine of a healthy, self-supporting Jewry of which the greater Jewry may well be proud, an object of admiration to all outside of Jewry.

Thus both Jews and Arabs—the extremists, the political

THE NEXT STEP

nationalists are ignored—require individual freedom and communal or national—in the sense of nationality not nation—liberty, with security against interference or domination by any outside individual or body. The Jews in addition require a population of such dimensions as to constitute them absolutely and relatively a people and not merely a group—a healthy body by which their soul—the Jewish civilization, and culture—can be clothed and protected. Quite independent of Zionism, but connected by force of circumstances with Palestine, they require also a land of refuge for some of their tortured friends and kinsmen elsewhere. Above all the general welfare of the country is a necessity for all of them. In its absence neither Arab nor Jewish community or nationality can survive, except as a sink of hopeless poverty, or groups of dependants on charity. Putting aside for the moment the subject of Palestine as a land of refuge, these two requirements are not irreconcilable. Both Jew and Arab can have full liberty as a man and as a Jew or Arab. A Jewish community of an adequate size, both absolutely and relatively, can grow up in Palestine without threatening the position of the Arabs. Jewish culture—the Jewish National Home in the sense of Ahad Ha'Am, Dr. J. L. Magnes and the other wisest thinkers among the Zionists—can be safeguarded. And neither the Jews nor the Arabs need run the risk of being dominated by the other. And all this can be effected within the framework of the Statement of Policy of May 1939. But to secure this end the policies of an Arab State in Palestine and of its counterpart a Jewish State must both be abandoned. The Statement of Policy states that Palestine shall be constituted a sovereign independent (Palestinian) State within a reasonable period of time. All Palestinians—irrespective of race or religion or origin—will become citizens of this State. They will be equal politically, civilly and in all other respects. No circumstances will give one an advantage over the other. In all matters over which the legislature, in the choice of which every citizen will have similar powers, has jurisdiction, all Palestinians will be equal. In this respect, to vary Dr. Weizmann's phrase, Jews and Arabs in Palestine will be as Palestinian as English and Scottish in Britain are British. When the Legislative Council is established, and this might well be before independence becomes a fact, it would be well, if it is agreed that it should deal only with those matters that concern Palestinians as Palestinians and not as Jews or Arabs, that the constituencies should be based on geography not community. A similar reform was introduced into municipal government in 1934 and helped to relieve the intercommunal feeling in the mixed municipalities.

The Central Government and the Legislative Council can deal only with matters that concern all elements in the population in common. In Palestine, as in other eastern lands, even in Europe, there are matters perhaps, probably of greater importance, that concern the inhabitants not in common but only as members of their special community. This was recognized in the old Ottoman constitution and is also to some extent recognized in the present law of Palestine. This latter legislation has enabled a General Council of the Jews of Palestine—similar councils can be constituted by the Moslems and other communities—to be set up which has considerable powers in such matters as marriage, divorce, inheritance, religion, education. In fact in these matters

THE NEXT STEP

the Jewish community has complete self-government. These powers might be extended to cover other fields—social legislation, labour regulations when both employers and employees are Jews, education so far as the withheld powers are concerned or most of them and others. The Arabs and the Jews both chafe under the present Government control, limited so far as the Jews are concerned, over education. Education—certainly elementary and secondary education—might well be left to the communities to manage in their own way and to pay for out of their own pockets, with subventions on a capitation basis from the Central Government. Such education might be good or bad, limited or universal, paid or free. The Central Government would have no responsibility for it and could not therefore be blamed.

Similarly with labour legislation, Jews or Arabs could introduce a minimum age of employment for their own children or not as they felt inclined and could see that the law was observed. They could lay down their own maximum hours of labour. The Central Government would have no responsibility and no concern. Jews, and similarly Arabs, could have their own courts to deal with and administer their own law in matters of civil litigation so long as both litigants were Jewish or Arab. Even in mixed cases these courts could act if the non-Jewish or non-Arab party agreed. And judging from the experience when Palestine was still a part of the Ottoman dominions and the Jews were permitted to have unofficial courts to deal with such matters there would be instances in which Arabs at any rate would be willing to accept Jewish jurisdiction. But this of course would have to be entirely voluntary. Only when Jew took proceedings against Jew, at any rate in a civil matter, would the case go as a matter of course to a Jewish court.

Jews and Arabs are to a large extent segregated in Palestine. Even in Jerusalem, Haifa and Tiberias there are compact Jewish quarters in which not an Arab is to be found, and similarly no Jew lives in an Arab quarter. Even Christian and Moslem Arabs keep similarly apart in social life, while the Armenians, the Bahais, the Druses, and the other smaller communities are also self-contained, residentially at any rate. It would in these circumstances be quite practicable to give Jews and Arabs a wide measure of municipal self-government at the cost of putting insignificant numbers of either community under the municipal government of the other. In municipal matters also one of the Jewish grievances is the interference of the Central Government. If municipal government were relieved of some of the shackles of central control, as has been recommended by the Royal Commission, one of the grievances of the Jews would be removed. They might be given very wide autonomy, the responsibility for success or failure resting with them, the Central Government stepping in only when other interests are concerned, for instance in the administration of preventive medicine as distinct from curative. This municipal autonomy might be extended to some extent to the Jewish quarters of mixed municipal areas for which there is already provision in the Municipalities Ordinance. The general services granted by the Municipality may be supplemented by the inhabitants of any ward or group of wards at their own expense. Jewish municipalities could co-operate, even combine, with neighbouring Jewish municipalities or village councils and thus form counties entirely inhabited by Jews and practically independent of outside control in municipal matters. Here would be Jewish cantons, not one canton which is impracticable without placing Arabs under Jewish government, but several smaller cantons or counties.

With complete autonomy in matters of education, religion, personal status, social legislation and municipal government, with liberty to live their own lives, administer their own laws and develop their own culture, much if not all the Jewish National Home as envisaged by Ahad Ha'Am, most of his predecessors and many of his successors, would be attained. Even in his moment of elation, almost ecstasy, when he appeared before the Supreme Council of the Allies in Paris in February 1919, Dr. Weizmann seems to have contemplated something of this nature, at any rate for that generation.

> 'The Zionist Organisation did not want an autonomous Jewish government, but merely to establish in Palestine, under a Mandatory Power, an administration, not necessarily Jewish, which would render it possible to send into Palestine 70,000 to 80,000 Jews annually. The Organisation would require to have permission at the same time to build Jewish schools, where Hebrew would be taught, and to develop institutions of every kind. Thus it would build up gradually a nationality, and so make Palestine as Jewish as America is American or England, English. Later on, when the Jews formed the large majority, they would be ripe to establish such a Government as would answer to the state of the development of the country and to their ideals.'[1]

[1] Lloyd George, *The Truth About the Peace Treaties*, pp. 1158–9.

Balfour himself seems to have had a similar ideal before him,[1] which can also be read into the famous Churchill White Paper. Historically also a National Home in this form would be in the direct succession from the Council of the Four Lands and the Lithuanian Council of the sixteenth, seventeenth and eighteenth centuries, perhaps the happiest period in the history of East European Jewry.

General Nuri es Said, in the scheme for a settlement that he put forward in October 1938, included one of communal and municipal autonomy such as this. If not avowedly, he was certainly in effect speaking in the names of all of the Arab rulers, and if the proposals had been pursued at the time it is not improbable that the agreement of the Palestinian Arab leaders could also have been obtained. Mr. George Antonius, a member of the Arab Delegation to the abortive conference and generally believed to be one of the most valuable advisers of the Palestinian Arab leaders, made a similar proposal.[2] He envisaged a treaty between Britain and the proposed Palestinian State with a provision 'affording the Jewish community the widest freedom in the pursuit of their spiritual and cultural ideas'.

Under any Palestine constitution the Jews would be and would probably, at any rate for many years, remain in a minority. If they ceased to be a minority the Arabs would become one. Some safeguards for a minority would therefore be necessary in any circumstances. The best and only completely effective safeguard is the sense of fairness and justice of the majority. This holds in all countries, for everywhere

[1] See p. 96.
[2] *The Arab Awakening*, p. 410.

there are minorities even if they are not racial. Fairness, justice and goodwill cannot, however, be created by act of parliament. They must grow of themselves. It is, however, possible to draft safeguards that would be effective so far as civilized peoples or those that have any desire to be considered civilized are concerned. And in drawing up a constitution, safeguards, even if there were no real need for them, are desirable. The greatest safeguard of all in the case of Palestine would be Britain, which, mandate or no mandate, will continue as protector and as such must have great indirect if not direct influence on the Government, no matter what form it might take. So long as Palestine is in the last instance dependent on Britain for its existence as an independent State, Britain's wishes, even in matters of internal government, must carry great weight and Britain's influence will inevitably always be on the side of justice for the Jewish and all other nationalities. In fact, there is in the White Paper an implied British protection for these nationalities or communities. 'His Majesty's Government will require to be satisfied that in the treaty contemplated . . . adequate provision has been made for . . . the protection of the different communities in Palestine . . . and for the special position in Palestine of the Jewish National Home.'

These moral safeguards are considerable and very valuable, but it is agreed that still more is required. Formalists will want something in legal form as binding and extensive as it is possible to make a document binding and extensive. The constitution, including the declaration that all Palestinian citizens are free and equal and laying down the communal and municipal independence that has been foreshadowed, would be formulated in an instrument, which as is usual with such instruments could not be varied by less than say two-thirds of the members of the legislative body. The Jewish population is about one-third of the total population of the country and its representation in the legislative body would be at least one-third. In this event the representatives of the Jews, although of themselves unable to carry legislation, would have the power to veto any change in the constitution. It is possible to go even further. Britain is and will continue to be in a special position in regard to the Holy Places, the communities, defence. Any change in the constitution that would affect these would be a British interest. Britain as it is would have the right to veto any proposal bearing on the defence or foreign relations of the country. It might be given a similar veto regarding the communities, a veto going so far as to prohibit even the introduction into the legislature of any proposal to alter the constitution under this head without its prior consent.

The foregoing suggestions indicate in a sense a move forward. Accompanying or following closely on them might be another move which would to some extent be backward. For almost two thousand years, with only brief intervals, Palestine has been a part of a greater entity. Since the expulsion of the Egyptians at the end of the thirteenth century it has formed one or more administrative districts of a province of an empire. For an independent Palestine one has to go back to King Solomon, except for the time of the Latin Kingdom when it was in a sense a European colony, dependent always on assistance from Europe. Economically Palestine has not for centuries been able to live alone and the experience of the past twenty years does not suggest that it will be able, especially as an industrial country with a relatively large population, to live alone to-day. Diplomatically there is even less possibility. Without protection from outside, Palestine in a world constituted as it is, would exist as an independent or semi-independent State for at the most a few months. In both respects Syria and the Lebanon State are in a similar position and as for Iraq, Britain there also alone stands between the State and subjection to a foreign power. In fact the era of small and weak States anywhere has passed. The lesson of Central Europe, of the separation of the Austro-Hungarian Empire into independent fragments, emphasizes this. And economically also small States cannot stand alone. There is no one to-day who does not regret the absence of provision in the Treaties of St. Germain' and the Trianon for at least an economic federation between the Succession States. The absence of such a provision helped towards the miseries from which the peoples of Central Europe suffered for two decades and to the cataclylsm by which they were ultimately overwhelmed. If Palestine and also Transjordan, Syria and the Lebanon are to have any chance of a peaceful and prosperous future it is essential that politically and economically they should be brought much closer. It is perhaps desirable that Iraq also should be brought into such a confederation or federal State.[1]

Before the Balfour Declaration and other instruments came to the knowledge of the Arabs there was not one

[1] According to Thomas Raleigh 'International lawyers distinguished between a federal State, all parts of which are represented, for international purposes, by one government, and a confederation of States, whose governments retain the right to be separately represented and considered.'

of them to whom the idea of a political separation between Syria and Palestine, or Northern and Southern Syria as they still call the two countries, had occurred as a possibility. Syria was and always had been an indivisible whole. To separate it into parts would be an act of violence that no one could contemplate. Consistently, from the visit of the King-Crane Commission and earlier, the Arabs asked for an integral Syria. It might be under British or American or even French protection, but that it was to be one and undivided was always a cardinal principle. In so far as Jewish settlement in Palestine with powers of self-government was ever thought of by Feisal or any other Arab leader it was always as a part of a greater federal State. And the Zionists of the Balfour Declaration were not averse to the same suggestion. A Jewish National Home, even a sort of Jewish State, as a part of a Greater Syria; Yes. Otherwise; No. The Pan-Arab Congress of Jerusalem of December 1931 went even further. The 'covenant' which it adopted declared that *the Arab lands were a 'complete and indivisible whole'* and that all efforts should be directed towards their complete independence, and when the Arab Independence Party was formed a few months later, a Pan-Arab State, comprising Palestine, Transjordan, Iraq and Syria, was the principal plank in its platform.

Apart, however, from political and economic reasons, there is also a very strong desire for some sort of union on the part of the peoples living north and south of the present Palestinian boundary. Such a union has also been one of the desiderata of the Arab politicians who always refused to recognize what they considered an unnatural separation. In fact the political boundary

THE NEXT STEP

cuts a people in half. The inhabitants of Beyrout and of Haifa are one, in many cases closely related. The lands of some of the Northern Palestine villages are to-day in Syria and those of Syrian villages in Palestine. A frontier runs between the two countries but so that the villagers may live means have had to be adopted to enable them to pass freely to and fro without the hindrance of passport regulations. Similarly with regard to Transjordan. From time immemorial the Bedouin of Transjordan have been accustomed at the appointed seasons to wander with their flocks and their herds into Palestine. They know of no hindrance to a continuation of this practice and cannot recognize or realize such a hindrance. Thus the frontier between Palestine and Transjordan has had to be left open for the inhabitants to come and go, but seldom stay.

The advantages of a federation of the neighbouring States was recognized by Dr. Weizmann and other Zionist thinkers almost from the day on which Zionism became practical politics. Such a federation was, to say the least, not ruled out by the negotiations between Dr. Weizmann and the Amir Feisal, afterwards King of Iraq, in the period immediately following the issue of the Balfour Declaration. In such a federation, a Jewish National Home, even a Jewish Federal State, could offer no threat. Dr. Weizmann realized the wisdom, the advantage from the Jewish point of view, of the inclusion of Palestine in such a federation and of the consequent silencing of much prospective hostility. A little later, in 1923, Hussein, then King of the Hedjaz, was generally believed to favour a federation of Arab States including Palestine, with special reservations in favour of a Jewish National Home there. Lord Samuel, who with regard to Palestine combines wisdom with experience, when castigating the Royal Commission's recommendations in the House of Lords, indicated an alternative solution in the direction of federation. Dr. Weizmann may not have realized in full how the existence of a Jewish population in Palestine must be dependent on industry. To-day only some thirteen or fourteen per cent of the Jewish population live by agriculture or horticulture. The alternatives before the present population are either foreign markets or support from abroad, and as time passes the choice of alternative becomes more insistent.

The Jews of Palestine are dependent on foreign markets and the nearest and most obvious and easiest attainable are those in the neighbouring lands. Federation would give them a secure market, whose exploitation would rest in their hands entirely, except for other internal competition. Without federation, or at any rate a complete liquidation of the present mutual attitude, these markets are largely closed. Politics in the Middle East spreads at once into all departments of life and many amateur politicians are, it seems, always prepared to boycott their neighbours and opponents, even if by doing so they harm themselves. Here again with or without federation the future of the Jews of Palestine is dependent on their relations with the Arabs.

One large federal State of which Palestine would form a part would bring with it yet a further advantage in the present complicated circumstances. Of all the problems with which the Palestinian statesman is confronted those of immigration and land purchase are the most obstinate. Here indeed are the irresistible force and the immovable body. In viewing the constitutional difficulties glimmers of light sometimes appear. The satisfaction of the immigration and land needs of the two parties are invariably lost in cimmerian darkness. The new immigration policy lays down a 'political high level' for Jewish immigration, independent of all estimates of economic absorptive capacity. This latter criterion has certainly not worked perfectly in the past and it is evident that the immigration has sometimes exceeded, not fallen below, economic absorptive capacity. But the answer to this failure is the provision of more satisfactory machinery and the purely scientific handling of it. Theoretically economic absorptive capacity is the best criterion: to introduce political considerations may relieve the political situation but cannot bring all possible economic benefit. If the country needs and can benefit by having more blacksmiths or tailors or industrial capitalists, it should have them. In present circumstances and in a self-contained Palestine whose Arab inhabitants are without cessation haunted by the fear of domination, the restriction of Jewish immigration, justified or unjustified, is inevitable. The same is the case with regard to land purchase. The safeguarding of the small cultivator, whether owner or tenant, and also of the landless agricultural labourer is essential. Article VI of the Mandate implies the safeguarding of the interests of these small cultivators. 'The Adminstration of Palestine, *while ensuring that the rights and position of other sections of the population are not prejudiced*[1] ... shall encourage ... close settlement by Jews on the land.' It is by this Article that much of the land legislation of Palestine has been inspired. It is desirable, if only in the interests of the community as a whole, that

---

[1] The italics are mine.

a large uprooted population, removed with or without compensation from the land on which it was born and without which it cannot maintain itself, even if driven into the ranks of casual labour in the cities, should not become a permanent danger to the whole community. But land legislation that differentiates against one section of the community, especially by name, is entirely alien to British practice. It is a system that can bring no satisfaction to any Englishman.

With Palestine, however, a part of a larger federation, immigration and land-owning would fall into their proper relative positions. There can never be any possibility of a Jewish majority in the population of such a larger State, and if the Jews happen to become a majority in one portion of it, in a corner, even if they gain control of its local government the position of the Arabs and other communities in the State as a whole cannot be threatened. The Government that counts is the Central Government. In that not one or even two federal States will have control. The electorate will be wider and larger. The Jews of Palestine, like the Maronites of the Lebanon, would have their share in that Central Government, but they would not monopolize it. It might happen that in the central legislature Jews and Maronites and Shiahs and Sunnis might as time passed forget their distinctive communities and differences and find themselves grouped in political parties. In Palestine already while relations between Jew and Arab were still strained almost to breaking point economic misfortunes have made them forget their mutual antipathies and work together for the common weal. In a federal State, whose parliament would legislate only on general questions common to all communities and could have no concern with communal matters, Jews and Arabs might at length discover that they are Syrians or Palestinians as well as Jews and Arabs, just as a common national policy has bridged the centuries-old separation between Christian and Moslem. Similarly with regard to land. Safeguard the cultivator. Render his future secure, so far as it is possible to render it secure. Then let every inhabitant or at any rate every citizen be free to acquire whatever land he wishes, and if Jews wish to buy waste or uncultivable land and change its nature, why hinder them? If they fail they will be the only losers: if they succeed not only they but the whole community must benefit. Never can the Jews or any other of the smaller sections of the population acquire the greater part of the land of the whole State. The majority need never fear that they as a community will be expropriated. On the acquisition of land no conditions that could not be justified should be imposed. The man who is dependent on his holding must be safeguarded. Otherwise land not held in trust should be available for purchase by any purchaser, without limitation except perhaps of citizenship. Leases and tenancies also should not be limited to members of any one community or another. And the employment or non-employment of any class of citizen should not be made the condition of any lease or tenancy. All citizens should in all matters be free and equal.

To return for a moment to immigration. Under the recent White Paper, the Jewish population is to rise in the course of the next ten years, mainly by means of immigration, to a third of the whole population. At the end of the ten years, if there is then no further immigration, the Jewish proportion in the population will in the absence of emigration of the non-Jewish portion begin to fall, for the rate of natural increase of the Jews in Palestine as elsewhere is lower than that of the surrounding population. The Jewish immigrants enter against the will of the Arabs. Elsewhere, in Iraq, Egypt, Syria, where the Arabs have power, Jewish immigration is prohibited, partly as a reflexion of the anti-Jewish feeling in Palestine, partly out of fear of possible Jewish political designs if given the opportunity. Even the situation in Palestine could be relieved, if the fear and suspicion of the Jew were to pass away, and both these motives would disappear. Arab statesmen admit that they need certain classes of immigrants and that the Jews could supply them, that the advent of Jewish immigrants would increase the prosperity of their countries. At the moment they are afraid to admit them. Remove this fear and with or without federation new lands of settlement and happiness would be opened for some of the refugees from European brutalities whose friends are so hard put to find them resting-places. And it must not be thought that Jews alone would benefit by immigration into this larger federal State or any of its parts. Elsewhere Jewish and other refugee populations have built up wealth in the lands of the Old World as well as the New. The Arab lands are at present in the earliest years of their re-birth and an immigrant Jewish population, especially one of the cultural level of those of the German lands, could and would help much in building up cultural, intellectual and also material wealth. A prosperous Jewish community would bring prosperity to the other communities of the land and in them the whole country would prosper. After all, the prosperity of the whole consists of the prosperity of the parts. A happy Jewish National Home in Palestine or elsewhere would help to make the parallel Arab National Home also happy.

Hostility between Arab and Jew or Moslem and Jew is not one of the fixed conditions of history. There have been periods of intense hostility and hatred but despite them the history during the past millenium of Arab or Moslem and Jew compares favourably with that of European or Christian and Jew. Many a time Jewish fugitives from Christian or European persecution have found a refuge and a welcome in Moslem and in Arab lands. The Jews as non-Moslems until very recent times, in Turkey and Egypt for instance, were at the best second-class citizens, but in this respect and for the same reason they were no worse off than Christians. The Moslems were the lords but the subjects might still live in tolerable comfort. This was in the material sphere. There was another one in which Jew and Arab were more equal. In the great period of Arab intellectual history when Europe was still in a twilight, the light of the world came from the Arab lands. Then and in that period the literature, the thought, the culture were Arabic, but the men and the minds behind that culture, those that breathed into it the breath of life, were Jews equally with Arabs. Is another such period of intellectual co-operation inconceivable?

INDEX

Abdullah, Amir, 179–80.
Abrahams, Israel, 13.
Advisory Council, 138, 139.
Agricultural Settlement, Jewish, 30 et seq., 47 et seq., 122, 125.
Ahad Ha'Am, 13, 61–3, 86, 94, 108–12, 160, 193.
Alien Immigration Commission, 73.
Alkalay, Judah, 56.
Alliance Israélite Universelle, 52.
American Zionists, 90, 97–8.
Ancient Maccabaeans, Order of, 115.
Anglo-Jewish Association, 53.
Anglo-Palestine Bank, 118.
Anti-Semitism, 65–6.
Antonius, Mr. George, 103, 104.
The Arab Awakening, 104, 198.
Arab Agency, 138.
Arab Congresses, 180, 202.
Arab Higher Committee, 169, 171.
Arab Independence Party, 202.
Arab-Jewish Relations, 139, 143, 209.
Arab Outbreaks, 121, 131, 140–1, 148, 168–70, 179.
Arab Position, 95–7, 102, 133.
Arab Revolt, The, 89, 102.
Arab State, An, 160, 193.
Arab Sympathy, Foreign, 148, 170–1, 179–80.
Arabs, Britain and the, 86, 103–4, 159–60.
Arish, El, Project, 73, 74.
Armenian Problems, 86.
Artuf, 60.
Ashe, Isaac, 45.
Ashley, Lord, see Lord Shaftesbury.
Association for Promoting Jewish Settlements in Palestine, 37, 53.

Balfour, Lord, 86, 95–6, 102, 163.
Balfour Declaration, The, 90 et seq., 129, 132–3, 154, 198.

Balfour Declaration, Motives of, 97 et seq., 104 et seq., 154.
Bar Cochba, 19, 46.
Basle Programme, 70.
Bene Moshe, 62, 63.
Benisch, Abraham, 52–3.
Benjamina, 59.
Berlin Congress, 154.
Bible cited, 7–8, 9, 148.
Bicheno, James, 27, 28.
Bilu, 60.
Bludan Congress, The, 180.
B'nai B'rith, Independent Order, 60.
Bohemia, Persecution of Jews in, 154.
Bolshevism, Jews and, 98–9.
Bonar, Andrew, 48.
Bradshaw, S. A., 44.
Brandeis, Justice L. D., 92.
Britain, Jews and, 88, 106, 157–9.
British Consulate in Jerusalem, 28–9, 30.
British Interest in the Jews, 27, 31–3, 73 et seq., 153 et seq.
British Interest in Palestine, 27, 31–3, 88.
British Jews and Palestine, 71, 73, 100–1.
British Protection of Jews, 50.
Bukeah, 47–8.

Cabinet, A Jewish, 91.
Canning, Lord, 52.
Cazalet, Edward, 41–2.
Cecil, Viscount, 99, 104.
Chamberlain, Joseph, 74.
Chancellor, Sir John, 140, 147, 149.
Chovevé Zion, 56, 58, 60–3, 67, 68, 70, 80.
Church of Scotland, General Assembly of the, 33.
Churchill, Col. Charles Henry, 43.
Churchill White Paper, 131, 132 et seq., 139, 143, 166, 184–5, 198.
Churchill, Mr. Winston, 112, 149, 152, 155, 163–4.

Civil Servants, British, 161, 174.
Clarke, Dr. Thomas, 45.
Columbus, Christopher, 18.
Communal Self-Government, 194–6.
Conder, Major Claude, 42.
Conference, The London, 183–4.
Constitutional Safeguards, 198 et seq.
Council of the Four Lands, 198.
Cox, Sir Henry, 170.
Crémieux, Adolphe, 34.
Cresson, Warder, 37–8, 53–4.
Cromer, Earl of, 96.
Cromwell, Oliver, 20–1.
Crybbace, T. T., 44.
Curzon, Marquess, 96, 104, 155.

Dagania, 60.
Damascus Blood Accusation, 33-5.
Dönmeh, 25.
Dreyfus, Alfred, 65.

East Africa Project, 74–8.
Economic Dependence, 204.
Eder, M. D., 81.
Edward VII, King, 38.
Ekron, 59.
Employment of Jews, 124.
England, Re-settlement of Jews in, 20–2.
Ezra Society, Berlin, 60.

Federal State, A, 200 et seq.
Feisal, King, 203.
Finn, James, 30, 37.
France and Palestine, 88–9, 126.
Friedlander, M., *The Jewish Religion*, 17n.

Gaster, Moses, 71, 79, 83, 87, 94.
Gawler, Col. George, 35–7, 51.
Ginzberg, Asher, see Ahad Ha'Am.
Goldsmid, Sir I. L., 100.
Gottheil, Richard, 71.
Great Britain and Palestine, 1915–1939 cited, 190.
Greenberg, Leopold J., 87.
Gutmacher, Elijah, 52, 56.

Haas, Jacob de, 91–2.
Haas, de, and Wise, *The Great Betrayal*, 93.

Hadassah Organization, 115.
Harlech, Lord, 177.
Hebrew Christians, 4, 60.
Hebrew, Definition of, 6.
Hebrew, Status of, 125.
Hedera, 59.
Herzl, Theodor, 63, 64–81, 92, 117.
Hess, Moses, 56.
Hexter, Dr. Maurice, 121.
Hillel, 10.
Hogarth Message, The, 102–3, 130.
Holy Places, The, 88, 185, 200.
House of Commons, 152, 162, 163–5.
House of Lords, 95, 163.
Hulda, 60.
Hussein, King, 102, 103, 104, 203

Ica, see Jewish Colonization Association.
Immigration into Palestine, 123, 139, 147, 166, 185–6, 208.
Immigrants, Selection of, 123–4, 132, 137, 139.
Immigration Policy, 205, 207–8.
India, Reactions in, 149, 171, 180.
International Hebrew Christian Alliance, 4.
Iraq, Government of, 179.
Israelite, Definition of, 6.
Italy, King of, 73.
Ito, see Jewish Territorial Organization.

Jabotinsky, Vladimir, 131, 147.
Jew, Definition of, 1–6.
Jewish Agency, 119–22, 143, 181.
Jewish Colonial Trust, 118.
Jewish Colonization Association, 58, 60.
Jewish *Encyclopedia* cited, 2.
Jewish National Fund, 72, 117.
Jewish National Home, 90 et seq., 108 et seq., 133, 134, 185, 192, 193, 197 et seq.
Jewish Race, 3.
Jewish State, A, 160, 175–6, 178, 181, 193.
Jewish Territorial Organization, 81.
Joint Foreign Committee, 113.

INDEX

Joseph, Morris, *Judaism as Creed and Life*, 5, 8.
Josippon, 153.
Judaism, Messianic, 16 et seq.
Judaizers, 22.
Judenstaat, Der, 66–7.

Kalischer, Hirsch, 52, 56.
Katrah, 60.
Kenya, see East Africa Project.
Keren Hayesod, 117–8.
King-Crane Commission, 159.
Kitchener, Lord, 48.

Land Legislation, 143, 145, 186–7, 205–6, 207.
Land Purchase, 117. See also Land Legislation.
Lansdowne, Lord, 74–5.
Lawrence, T. E., 94, 104.
League of Nations, Council of the, 126, 132, 155, 162, 166, 179, 185.
Legislative Council, 132, 138–9, 140, 143, 147, 149–52, 165, 194.
Lindsay, Lord, 29.
Lloyd-George, Mr. D., 85, 95, 96, 98, 99, 102, 106, 107, 155, 165.
London, Herzl in, 71, 73.
Lost Ten Tribes, 21.
Louis of Zion, see Chovevé Zion.

Maccabaeans, The, 71.
Macdonald Letter, The, 145–6, 165.
Macdonald, Mr. Malcolm, 183.
Macdonald White Paper, 184–5, 189, 199.
MacDonogh, Sir George, 99.
Magnes, Dr. J. L., 193.
Manasseh ben Israel, 21–2.
Mandate for Palestine, The, 119, 126 et seq., 154, 164, 174 et seq., 179, 205.
Mandates Commission of League of Nations, 155, 162, 165–7, 178–9.
Marmorek Brothers, The, 71.
Marshall, Louis, 121.
Mattuck, Rabbi I. I., *What are the Jews?*, 69–70.

M'Cheyne, Robert Murray, 48.
Mehemet Ali, 34–5, 49.
Melchett, 1st Lord, see Mond, Sir Alfred.
Messiahs, False, 19.
Metulla, 59.
Mikveh Israel, 51–2.
Millenarians, 21, 22.
Mission of Israel, 7–15, 69.
Mitford, E. L., 44–5.
Mizrachi Organization, The, 72, 115.
Mond, Sir Alfred, 96, 121.
Montefiore, Sir Moses, 34–5, 43, 48, 49–51, 100.
Municipal Self-government, 196–7.
Murray, Sir Archibald, 91.

Napoleon and the Jews, 28.
Nasi, Don Joseph, 48–9.
Netter, Charles, 52.
"Non-Zionists, The," 94, 112–13, 119, 121.
Nordau, Max, 71, 79.
Nuri es-Said, General, 198.

Oliphant, Laurence, 38–41.
Ormsby-Gore, Hon. W., see Harlech, Lord.
Oxford English Dictionary cited, 1–2.

Palestine cited, 91.
Palestine, British Projects for Settlement in, 30 et seq.
Palestine Colonization Fund, 51, 53.
Palestine Exploration Fund, 42.
Palestine—a Land of Refuge, 192, 193.
Palestine Jewish Colonization Association, 59.
Palmerston, Lord, 29, 30.
Pardes Anna, 59.
Partition, 175 et seq.
Partition Commission, The, 181–2.
Passfield White Paper, 143–5, 146, 155, 165.
Peel Royal Commission, 171 et seq.
Pekiin, 47–8, 49.
Petach Tikva, 51, 59.

Plumer, Lord, 149.
Pope, The, 73.
Population, Jewish, of Palestine, 123, 124, 147
Priestley, Joseph, 27.
Quarterly Review, 29, 32.
Rabbis and Zionism, The, 72.
Rishon le-Zion, 57, 59.
Rosh Pina, 57.
Rothschild, 1st Lord, 73.
   2nd Lord, 96.
   Baron Edmond de, 39, 57-9.
   Mr. James de, 59.
   Baron Lionel de, 100.
Ruppin, Dr. Arthur, 121.
Russia, Jewish Influence in, 98-9.
   and Palestine, 88-9.
Russian Government, The, 55, 73.
   Persecutions, 55.

Salomons, Sir David, 100.
Samuel, Viscount, 85, 131, 138, 178, 203-4.
Schomer, A. S., *The Primary Cause of Anti-Semitism*, 3.
Scott, Charles Prestwich, 85.
Self-Government, 59, 194-7.
Shabbathai Zevi, 22-6.
Shaftesbury, Lord, 29, 31-2.
Shaw Commission, The, 141-2, 166.
Simpson, Sir John Hope, 142-3.
Sinai Peninsula, 73.
Snell, Lord, 141-2.
Sobotniki, 7.
Society for the Promotion of Jewish Agricultural Labour in the Holy Land, 37.
Sokolow, Nahum, 62, 86, 87, 91, 116.
   History of Zionism, 95.
Spectator, The, 36.
Stein, Mr. L. J., 97.
Storrs, Sir Ronald, 162.
Sultan of Turkey, The, 72.
Survey of International Affairs, 97.

Sykes, Sir Mark, 86, 87.
Sykes-Picot Agreement, 87-9.
Syria, 159, 169, 201 *et seq.*
Tel Aviv, 50, 122, 123, 125.
Theudas, 19.
Tiberias, 48.
Times, The, 29, 31-2, 61, 130, 157n.
Transjordan, 88, 134-5, 170.
Tschlenow, Jechiel, 87.

Uganda, see East Africa Project.
United States, Government of, 107, 126.
University, Hebrew, 42, 62, 84.

War of 1914, The, 83.
Warburg, Felix, 120.
Wauchope, Sir Arthur, 147-8, 149-52.
Weizmann, Dr. Chaim, 84-7, 99, 106, 107, 116, 119, 120, 129-30, 131, 145, 156-7, 160, 177, 180, 197, 203, 204.
William, Emperor, 72-3.
Wise, Dr. Stephen, see Haas, de, and Wise.
Witherby, Thomas, 27, 28.
Wolffsohn, David, 79.
Women's International Zionist Organization, 115.

Yale, Professor William, 94.

Zangwill, Israel, 71, 79, 81, 83, 91.
Zichron Jacob, 38-41, 57.
Zionism, Cultural, 69.
   Political, 64 *et seq.*, 82.
   Practical, 46 *et seq.*, 82, 116.
   Spiritual, 69, 97-8.
Zionist Congresses, 63, 70, 71-72, 73, 77, 78, 80, 114, 115-6, 120, 133, 180-1.
Zionist Executive, Provisional, 83, 91.
   Organisation, 70, 114 *et seq.*, 135, 177.
   Colonization by, 60.
Zionists and the Arabs, 156-7.

For Product Safety Concerns and Information please contact our EU representative GPSR@taylorandfrancis.com
Taylor & Francis Verlag GmbH, Kaufingerstraße 24, 80331 München, Germany

www.ingramcontent.com/pod-product-compliance
Lightning Source LLC
Chambersburg PA
CBHW062219300426
44115CB00012BA/2137